MW00783332

Praise for

Breaking the Wineglass,
Living a Spiritual Life Beyond Religious Boundaries

"Ordinarily we don't think of religion as something that restricts spiritual experience, but Vic Jenkins' book, *Breaking the Wineglass,* exposes the reality of that truth in a profound and practical way. He takes the reader on a journey of self-discovery: of becoming cognizant of the shadow one's past memories casts on our present experience, releasing their restricting influence, and integrating new life-embracing concepts into our consciousness. Along the way he skillfully reminds us of the many wise and insightful words that have come from spiritually minded teachers throughout the ages."

Alden Studebaker, author of *Wisdom for a Lifetime –*
How To Get the Bible Off the Shelf and Into Your Hands.

"*Breaking the Wineglass: Living a Spiritual Life Beyond Religious Boundaries* by Vic Jenkins is a thinking person's guidebook into the hinterlands of deep spirituality. Written with boundless energy and world-embracing scope, *Breaking the Wineglass* continues a long tradition of introspection and creative expression pioneered by great mystics of the East and West. Jenkins deftly weaves a multi-faith, multicultural pattern, blending Sufi mystics like Kabir, Jelaluddin Rumi, and Abu Yazid with Christian luminaries like Hildegarde of Bingen, Francis of Assisi, Teresa de Avila, and Martin Luther. He is as much at home with the atheistic philosopher Arthur Schopenhauer as he is with the God-intoxicated Meister Eckhart. With this little volume, spiritual pathfinder Vic Jenkins has offered 21st century humanity a new access point to the trail leading to the mystical life."

Thomas W. Shepherd, D.Min., author, *Friends in High Places*

"Vic Jenkins' new book *Breaking the Wine Glass* is a refreshing and insightful blend of mystical teachings from the world's religions, Jungian psychology, provocative anecdotes, and humorous stories, all converging upon simple yet powerful ideas. This book is a very readable and clear example of the new spirituality that is emerging in the world today; a spirituality that draws upon many traditions, new physics, and the archetypal ideas revealed by Carl Jung.

Rev. Jenkins has distilled a lifetime worth of spiritual studies into a few short chapters that have everyday application for more fulfilling life and wisdom for nudging the world into more peaceful ways. In this book you will find new ways of seeing life, new ways of relating to the world, insightful counsel regarding forgiveness, and, as Rev. Jenkins delightfully puts it, for "waging peace."

Rev. Jenkins has a facility for selecting quotations from a wide range of human thought and blending them together in ways that reveal deeper meaning. The book is lively, interesting, and practical. Each chapter is followed by helpful questions for reflection and discussion.

I have known Vic Jenkins for over 20 years and know him to be a man of sound character, spiritual dedication, and breadth and depth of knowledge. He also has a delightful sense of humor and knack for story-telling which come through in this book. His consciousness and personality subtly shine through without obscuring or distracting from the practical mysticism that is the primary subject of his book. I highly recommend this book for anyone who is ready to re-examine personal beliefs and assumptions, to "break the wineglass," and let the "breath of Spirit" transform them.

James Gaither, co-author, *The Essential Charles Fillmore*
Senior Minister
Unity Center of Practical Christianity

Breaking the Wineglass

Living a Spiritual Life Beyond Religious Boundaries

Vic Jenkins

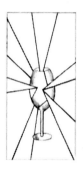

"Here's the new rule: Break the wineglass,
and fall toward the glassblower's breath."

- Jelaluddin Rumi

Ravenswood Court Publishing, a division of
James Stevenson Publisher

Copyright permissions:

Every effort has been made to trace copyright holders of material in this book. The author apologizes if any work has been used without permission and would be glad to be told of anyone who has not been consulted. Grateful acknowledgment is made for permission to reprint excerpts from the following:

"The New Rule" from *Open Secret: Versions of Rumi*, by John Moyne and Coleman Barks, Copyright © 1984 by John Moyne and Coleman Barks. Reprinted by arrangement with Shambhala Publications Inc., Boston, MA. www.shambhala.com.

Excerpts from *Pigs Eat Wolves* by Charles Bates. Copyright © 1991 by Yes Publishing Company.

Excerpt from "The Collective Unconscious" from *The Archetypes and the Collective Unconscious* by C. G. Jung, translated by R.F.C. Hull. Copyright ©1959 by Bollingen Foundation. New material copyright ©1969 by Princeton University Press.

Excerpt from *Avalanche* by W. Brugh Joy, M.D.. Copyright © 1990. Permission granted by author.

Quotes from *Owning Your Own Shadow* by Robert Johnson. Copyright © 1991 by Robert A. Johnson. Reprinted by permission of HarperCollins Publishers.

Excerpt from *The Sufi Message* by Hazrat Inayat Khan. Copyright © 1981 by East-West Publications.

Excerpt from *The Kingdom Within* by John Sanford. Copyright © 1970. Reprinted by permission of HarperCollins Publishers.

Jiménez' "I am not I...," from *Lorca & Jimenez* by Robert Bly. Copyright © 1973, 1997 by Robert Bly. Copyright © 1967 by The Sixties Press. Reprinted by permission of Beacon Press, Boston.

Rilke's "Ah, not to be cut off...," from *The Enlightened Heart: an Anthology of Sacred Poetry*, edited by Stephen Mitchell. Copyright © 1989 by Stephen Mitchell. Reprinted by permission of HarperCollins Publishers.

Excerpt, "There is no difficulty that enough love/...it all." from *Around the Year with Emmet Fox* by Emmet Fox. Copyright © 1958 by Harper & Brothers. Copyright renewed 1986 by Blanche Wolhorn and Kenneth A. Bro. Reprinted by permission of Harper Collins Publishers.

Brief quote, "Love is not a commodity to give... divine law." from *Life Is for Loving* by Eric Butterworth. Copyright © 1973 by Eric Butterworth. Reprinted by permission of HarperCollins Publishers.

"Love's Exquisite Freedom" by Maya Angelou. Copyright © 1996 by Maya Angelou. Reprinted by permission of The Helen Brann Agency, Inc.

Excerpt from "How to Tell a True War Story" from *The Things They Carried* by Tim O'Brien. Copyright © 1990 by Tim O'Brien. Reprinted by permission of Houghton Mifflin Harcourt Publishing Company. All rights reserved.

"The Peace of Wild Things," from *Collected Poems, 1957-1982* by Wendell Berry. Copyright © 1984 by Counterpoint Press.

Material from *Lessons in Truth* by Emily Cady, *The Mysteries of Genesis, The Twelve Powers of Man,* and *The Revealing Word,* by Charles Fillmore, *Healing Letters,* by Myrtle Fillmore, *The Story of Unity* by James Dillet Freeman, *The Quest* by Richard and Mary-Alice Jafolla, and *Myrtle Fillmore: Mother of Unity* by Thomas Witherspoon is used with permission of Unity, www.unity.org.

Scripture quotations from the *New Revised Standard Version* (NRSV). Copyright © 1989 by National Council of the Churches of Christ in the United States of America. Used by permission. All rights reserved.

Scripture quotations from the *New International Version* (NIV). Copyright © 1978 by New York International Bible Society. Used by permission of Zondervan. www.zondervan.com

The New Rule

It's the old rule that drunks have to argue and get into fights.
  The lover is just as bad: He falls into a hole.
But down in that hole he finds something shining,
  worth more than any amount of money or power.

Last night the moon came dropping its clothes in the street.
  I took it as a sign to start singing, falling *up* into the bowl of
  the sky.
The bowl breaks. Everywhere is falling everywhere.
  Nothing else to do.

Here's the new rule: Break the wineglass,
  and fall toward the glassblower's breath.

- Jelaluddin Rumi

To my daughter, Robin, (1963-2009)
who brought light and love
into so many lives

Breaking the Wineglass

Contents

Introduction and Acknowledgments

Cousin Richard taught me to play chess when most boys our age were playing baseball or participating in more hazardous physical activities. Richard, who was a couple of years older than I, had asthma and was often confined to the house. As a result, he read a lot and took to hobbies and pursuits different than the norm—like chess. He was the only chess player I knew.

Richard needed a partner. I seemed to be the most likely candidate, so he taught me to play. I learned the basics, the powers and limitations of each piece, as well as the importance of position and strategy. Soon, we were ready to play, or, more accurately, ready to *battle*.

A typical game of chess with Richard was one of merciless, ruthless mayhem. He would generously allow me to make the first move, and then, regardless of my move, he would proceed to swiftly and methodically annihilate my forces. Pawns, knights, bishops and queens were powerless before the onslaught. The carnage was devastating and complete. After several weeks of this, I found chess less than fascinating, and my thoughts turned to playing baseball with my buddies.

Then it happened. With the tally of victories standing at something like 67-0 in favor of Richard, I won! Interest renewed, my forces regrouped and commenced to compile another long series of humiliating defeats. This pattern continued. Richard would crush me, I would lose interest, and at the very moment I was ready to retreat to the world outside, I would somehow, amazingly, manage to win.

This was my introduction to grace, the kind of grace about which preachers talk, poets write, and musicians sing. Richard seemed invincible, I had no apparent chance of winning, and my life as a chess player appeared to be one long, pitiful road to failure. But just at the moment when things seemed hopeless, there would suddenly be a miraculous and uplifting victory that would once again encourage me to continue. I didn't know how to explain those infrequent and welcome victories.

But one day, during one of those grace-filled victories, Richard made a blundering move so uncharacteristic and obvious that I realized he was allowing me to win. It wasn't me, or grace, but Richard! Disillusioned, I returned to my friends and never played chess with him, or anyone else, for years. Grace, if it existed at all, had let me down.

Another fellow, interestingly, also named Richard, came into my life years later. We were in the same Army barracks, and he reintroduced me to chess. This time it was taught to me as an intricate and beautiful art form—less a competitive battle than an understanding of a cooperative, creative and dynamic interplay of power. The game stretched our minds and opened the doors to an appreciation of each other which went beyond strategy. Richard and I still kept score, but the beauty was not in who won or lost, or in the process of the game, but in our growing friendship. Grace had been there all along.

The common view of grace is that it is bestowed upon us, an infrequent, accidental occurrence—like winning the lottery. But grace is always beside us and within us. When we perceive life as a battle, it will *be* a battle, and there will be shattering defeats. But when we perceive the perfect pattern of life, we will see the beauty and grace in life—in defeat, as well as in victory.

As the years have passed, I have lost connection with the two Richards, who were my friends and teachers. That has been the case with numerous friends and mentors who have given me the privilege of being part of their journey. Their journey has been mine, and most, if not all, that is presented in this book is what we learned together. I am especially grateful for Teresa and John Stafford, who designed the cover. Jim Stevenson went beyond the call of duty in guiding me through the often puzzling intricacies of the publishing world. Life-long companions and support on this journey have been provided by my family, a remarkable collection of talented, compassionate and unusually sane folk. I began with three siblings, and over the years have accumulated dozens of brothers and sisters—all friends, all mentors. The sudden and tragic death of my daughter, Robin, opened the door to a deeper understanding of the ideas and beliefs expressed in this book. The loss of her physical presence has made my own lessons in forgiveness, peace—and love—especially relevant. Currently, I am most grateful for Jay and René, who, in addition to serving as teachers and friends, are absolutely the best sons I could imagine. Principal among all of these is my wife and my support, Carolynn, who is so giving in her wisdom and love that it is impossible to imagine her being absent from my life—Carolynn, full of grace.

This book primarily consists of articles written during the twenty years (1987-2007) I served as a Unity minister in Vacaville, California. Subtitled *Living a Spiritual Life Beyond Religious Boundaries,* the assumption is that our life journey is one of spiritual growth, and that all of our experiences hold great potential for learning and growth *if* we stay awake; every situation becomes a lesson, every person a teacher. In my own life, I have never strayed far from this belief. But in the course of my spiritual seeking, I wandered in and out of many religions—never finding quite the right fit. At the time, I thought they weren't ready for me. Now I have come to realize that I was not ready for *them.* The religious boundaries I came to embrace are found in the teachings of Unity—at the time of my ordination, Unity School of Christianity. The articles have been organized around seven chapters and will serve well as a seven-week study book—for individuals or groups. There are questions (*Inner Dialogue*) at the end of each chapter that may be used for group discussion. My prayer is that this book will lead each of you into a joyful appreciation of the gifts of grace at work in your own life.

Grace, my friends, demands nothing from us but that we shall await it with confidence and acknowledge it in gratitude.
- General Loewenhiem's speech from the film
Babette's Feast (1987)

Vic Jenkins
March 2010
Vacaville, California

Rule 1   The Breath

*"Here's the new rule: Break the wineglass, and
fall toward the glassblower's breath."*

- Jelaluddin Rumi (1207-1273)

What kind of rule is this? If we break the
wineglass, what happens to the wine? And   if
this is the new rule, what about the old rules? Are
they to be ignored? Are wineglasses obsolete?
What is Rumi suggesting? What does the wineglass represent, and who is the glassblower?
These are exactly the questions Rumi intended
to raise in any mind which conforms to boundaries and containers, which includes, I would
estimate, 99.99% of us. He is one in a long and
distinguished list of teachers—including
Buddha, Lao Tzu and Jesus of Nazareth—who
valued questioning easy answers. These are
teachers who broke the containers of conventional wisdom and explored a realm beyond
appearances, falling toward the presence of
spirit, "the glassblower's breath," at the essential core of life.

*Neither is new wine put
into old wineskins; other-
wise, the skins burst, and
the wine is spilled, and the
skins are destroyed; but
new wine is put into
fresh wineskins, and so
both are preserved.*

- Jesus of Nazareth
Matthew 9:17 (NIV)

When Jesus expressed the new rule, he spoke
of the need for new containers for the new wine.
However, he made it clear that he was not
concerned with breaking the old containers as
much as moving beyond them. "I do   not
come to abolish the law," he said, "but to fulfill
it." The "wineglasses" which contain our beliefs
and answers assume countless forms.   The
creeds and rules of church, school, political
party, labor union, indeed, of *any* movement in

which we choose to participate, become containers that embody and proscribe beliefs. Rumi says, as did Jesus centuries before, "Break the wineglass."

It is easy enough to break rules. There is a long list of the famous and infamous who have devoted their lives to breaking the rules. But there is an intriguing challenge posed by the phrase, "... fall toward the glassblower's breath." Again, the questions begin: Who is the glassblower? Why is the breath of the glassblower so important? How and why must we "fall" toward that breath? Asking these questions is to begin questioning answers that may have served in the past but are no longer enough. The wineglass that contained what I formerly believed to be true is no longer adequate. When Jesus said to his disciples, "I bring you food to eat that you know nothing about," he was referring to the "breath" that sustains life. That breath of Spirit is from the Source of being, the Creator's breath—or, as Rumi would say, the "glassblower's breath." Of the numerous faces and names that have been assigned God, "Glassblower" is most useful for my purposes in this book.

It is important to remember that the Glassblower creates an infinite number of shapes and forms, that the Glassblower's breath has been the source and inspiration of all those containers in our past, present, and future. By proclaiming a past container too small for the present is not

Do not think that I have come to abolish the law or the prophets; I have come not to abolish but to fulfill.

- Jesus of Nazareth
Matthew 5:17(NRSV)

Everything is full and pure at its source and precisely there, not outside.

- Meister Eckhart
[1260-1329]

to ignore its worth. The Christian church serves to demonstrate a wineglass frequently broken by those desiring to breathe more deeply of the Glassblower's breath. Hildegarde of Bingen, Francis of Assisi, Teresa de Avila, Meister Eckhart, Martin Luther, as well as Charles and Myrtle Fillmore, exemplify those who enlarged the container in order to experience a greater and deeper commitment to drinking directly from the Source. We recognize these mystics as our teachers, and at the core of their teachings was the belief that each of us is moving into a fuller consciousness of our connection with our Source—the "Glassblower."

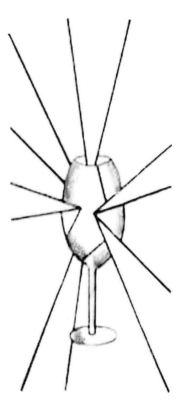

That is why you are reading these words now. You recognize that all that has occurred in your life has prepared you for this moment. You also undoubtedly sense that even though the shattered "wineglasses" in your past may have caused painful consequences, you have not only survived but have grown stronger as a result. The human willingness to break any container which restricts, confines or limits—the human yearning to move closer to the Source—is at the heart of our personal evolution as well as the spiritual evolution of the race. If this sounds a bit lofty, so be it! Our lives are not about trivial themes. As we consider and question the answers which we each bring into the container of our current lives, we confront issues involving forgiveness, love, compassion, and service. We find that past assumptions and beliefs may be questioned or even challenged. In some instances, this process may involve small-scale restructuring and release of former beliefs—easy enough to clean up. In other cases, the questioning may lead to considerable reevaluation and rebirth—a sometimes messy process involving considerable breakage. But always know, as you follow the "new rule," that you are part of a time-honored and ancient tradition. The container of another tradition holds that the "fall of man" involves shame and sin. The new rule considers the "fall" to be one of falling toward the breath of Spirit—toward a fulfillment of who we truly are. Jeremiah promised over 2600 years ago that there would some day be a new rule, one which, in his words, "would be written upon our hearts." This is a rule not to be contained in a wineglass, a book, a church, or a school—but *in our hearts*. He wrote, "No longer shall each man teach his neighbor and teach his brother, saying, 'Know God,' for they all shall know God…." Jesus spent his lifetime living and teaching the new rule. He was speaking of the "Glassblower's breath" when he spoke of Spirit (literally: "breath"), promising his disciples that when he left, the Spirit of truth would remain within each of them. Be assured that as you break the old containers you are a disciple of that Spirit of truth, willing to question and to breathe more deeply of life's essence.

I will put my law within them, and I will write it on their hearts. No longer shall they teach one another, or say to each other, 'Know the Lord,' for they shall know me, from the least of them to the greatest …

- Jeremiah 31:33-34 (NRSV)

I will ask the Father and he will give you another Advocate, to be with you forever. This is the Spirit of truth, whom the world cannot receive, because it neither sees him nor knows him. You know him, because he abides with you, and will be in you.

- Jesus of Nazareth
John 14:16-17 (NRSV)

Break the Wineglass containing the belief....
"I'm only human"
and fall towards
The Glassblower's Breath...
"I am a spiritual being living a
human experience.
I am free, I am unlimited!"

The Breath: Inner Dialogue

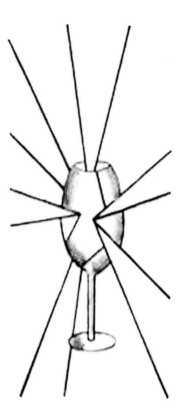

Considering the wineglass as a metaphor for beliefs that limit my spiritual understanding, which of my own wineglasses would I most want to break? Why?

Specifically, what keeps me from breaking these particular wineglasses? What do I gain from holding on to these beliefs?

How might my life change if I moved away from these patterns and beliefs that no longer serve me?

Describe a personal experience that involved "breaking a wineglass", an old pattern or belief. What was the result? What did I learn?

The Breath

Rule 2   Remembering

A time comes in our development when we need to take back what we and our culture have put in the darkness because some of what we have buried there is essential for our next steps.

- Charles Bates

Once upon a time, a man was out walking in the desert when a voice said to him, "Pick up some pebbles, put them in your pocket and tomorrow you will be both glad and sorry." The man obeyed. He stooped down and picked up a handful of pebbles, putting them in his pocket. The next morning he reached into his pocket and found diamonds, rubies and emeralds. And, truly, he was both glad and sorry. Glad that he had taken some… Sorry that he had not taken more.

We place all sorts of things into memory, with memory serving as "pockets" of consciousness. There are times when we reach into memory and realize that we have been carrying a treasure all along. And there are those times when it may seem as if our pockets are filled with the dead weight of worthless junk. But in the story, the voice is telling us that everything we pick up is of worth; if we want to be glad, we need to pick up as much as we can. To remember is to reach into the pockets of memory, to see all that we have accumulated on our walks through life.

We have within us, bound in the cage of the subconsciousness, all the propensities and the savagery of the animals ... These memories are part of the soul, and in the unregenerate they come to the surface sporadically. Sometimes whole nations seem to revert from culture to savagery without apparent cause, but there is always a cause. These reversions are the result of some violent wrenching of the soul, or of concentration, to the exclusion of everything else, on a line of thought out of harmony with divine law.

- Charles Fillmore

Here is a conundrum—a riddle—a mystery: We remember only those things of which we are conscious, but we don't forget anything. We remember everything. Those things we say we don't remember are actually filed away and stored in that area of consciousness we label "subconscious." When we say, "I forget," we really mean, "I can't find it," or, perhaps, "I don't want to find it." The truth is, we've been picking up everything and putting it all into the very deep pockets of memory, and after quite a walk, they are full. The crucial question for the man in the story, and for each of us, is this: "Of all of those things in your pocket, which are pebbles and which are gems?" What is useful and what is not? In the story, the pockets contained only gems, but in my own life story there have been not only pebbles but some real *boulders* along the way.

Remembering, or bringing conscious attention to the past, can be a painful experience. There are several time-honored methods of avoiding these painful memories. A personal favorite is to deny a painful event ever happened; not necessarily to overtly lie about it, but to block it from memory. Knowing what we know about memory, however, that is a great self-deception. Rather than "forgetting" it, I am actually "stuffing" it—back into the pocket with a tag attached saying, "Ignorance is bliss."

A second favored technique of avoiding painful memories is to run away from them.

If you bring forth what is within you, what you bring forth will save you. If you do not bring forth what is in you, what you do not bring forth will destroy you.

- Jesus of Nazareth
The Gospel of Thomas

Unlike the first technique, denial, this method involves attempting to escape and avoid altogether having to look at the memory. Whenever it threatens to make an appearance, I may refuse to look at it by changing the subject, or by substituting another experience in order to cover it up—keeping it in the pocket with an attached tag: "Out of sight, out of mind."

A third common response when painful memories are encountered is very different from the first two—denial and avoidance. Rather than forgetting, this response is to recall every minute detail of the past—to fret, worry and endlessly obsess—hoping to somehow change this pebble into a gem. Keeping it out of the memory pocket with a tag saying, "should have...," "could have...," or "if only..."

None of these methods work. They don't change the past. The past is still here whether we deny, run from, or obsess about it. We can't just say "forget it." We may try, but ultimately we must come to terms with our past. To truly "come to terms" with the past is to *heal*, to become whole, to remember that who we *were* is a part of who we *are*. An important step in doing this is to simply acknowledge that there is no such thing as forgetting. To get on with life, and to release the acquired baggage of the past requires challenging some widely accepted beliefs. The belief that forgetting is the equivalent of forgiving is not true and stands in the way of healing past and present.

If thou has not seen the devil,
look at thine own self.

\- Rumi

Obsessive remembrance, or living in the past, is very different from healing remembrance. The pocket full of gems alludes to healing remembrance. To be able to see the treasure inherent in the pebbles in the past does not mean to throw away the pebbles, but to *let go of the emotional attachment to past conditions and circumstances.* "Let go, let God," does not refer to letting go of the past conditions, but to letting go of our perceptions, beliefs, and emotions surrounding past events. "Let go, let God" means to acknowledge the anger, fear, shame or guilt of the past, and choosing to let it be replaced by love, compassion and peace—let good, or God, prevail.

This teaching is expressed in another way by writers of the Christian scriptures. In a remarkable sequence found in the gospel according to Matthew, Jesus is speaking of the kingdom of heaven to his followers. He is teaching them in the eastern tradition of parables, which require a great deal of thought and interpretation. When some of his followers asked why he insisted on using this difficult method of teaching, he replied that it was because the kingdom of heaven involved that which was hidden in the heart, in secret. The kingdom of heaven, Jesus said, is like a mustard seed, like yeast, like a treasure, and... like a *net,* which when cast into the sea draws fish of every kind. When drawn ashore, fishermen sort the useful and throw away those which are of no use.

I am not a mechanism, an assembly of various sections. And it is not because the mechanism is working wrongly, that I am ill. I am ill because of wounds to the soul, to the deep emotional self and the wounds to the soul take a long, long time, only time can help and patience, and a certain difficult repentance, long, difficult repentance, realization of life's mistake, and the freeing oneself from the endless repetition of the mistake which mankind at large has chosen to sanctify.

-    D. H. Lawrence

When we cast the net into the interior realm of consciousness, there are all sorts of memories to be drawn in and remembered. To be fully present to life is to draw them all in and to choose what is useful and what is not. Right now! Then we are able to continue the walk through life whole and complete.

There is a shadow clouding our memory, a shadow so great that it challenges powers of description. Because it is so hidden, the shadow is better sensed and felt, rather than seen and heard. Consequently, it is best described through the arts—music, sculpture, poetry— mediums which engage the emotional depths of being. So the shadow is often felt in remorse or regret—in poignant and bittersweet remembrances of what should, or could, have been. This shadow is so universal that it has been labeled with a capital "S" by Carl Jung and several generations of psychologists. At the beginning of the twentieth century, Jung described The Shadow as embedded in the deepest core of each human being, binding us together into one collective body.

Just as there is nothing lost in personal memory, so is there nothing lost in the memory of the collective. All of our past, the accumulated triumphs and tragedies of history, are present in human consciousness. The work of

In addition to our immediate consciousness, which is of a thoroughly personal nature... there exists a second psychic system of a collective, universal, and impersonal nature which is identical in all individuals. This collective unconscious does not develop individually but is inherited. It consists of pre-existent forms, the archetypes, which can only become conscious secondarily and which give definite form to certain psychic contents.

- Carl Jung

healing the pain and suffering on this planet requires an acknowledgment of the common bond of shared human history.

Anthony de Mello, in his wonderful book, *The Song of the Bird,* tells of a salt doll who journeyed for thousands of miles until it finally came to the sea. Fascinated by this strange, moving mass, unlike anything encountered before, the doll asked, "Who are you?" The sea smilingly replied, "Come in and see." So the doll walked in. The farther it walked into the sea, the more it dissolved, until there was very little of it left. Before that last bit dissolved, the doll exclaimed in wonder, "Now I know what I am!" Becoming conscious of who I am, knowing who *we* are, requires acknowledgment and immersion in the sea of the collective consciousness—returning home to the place of connection with the Creator. This is the home which Jesus called the kingdom of heaven.

While he was still far off, his father saw him and was filled with compassion; he ran and put his arms around him and kissed him ... this brother of yours was dead and has come to life; he was lost and has been found.

- the Prodigal Son returns home
Luke 15:20 & 32 (NRSV)

While taking his customary evening walk, a man happens to pass the home of a friend. He is startled to see, in front of the house underneath the street light, his friend on hands and knees searching for something. "Did you lose something?" he asks. "My car keys," is the reply. Wanting to be helpful, he suggests,

"Perhaps you left them somewhere else." "Actually," his friend answers, "I dropped them over there by the driveway." "Then why," he exclaims, "are you looking for them here?" His friend shrugs and answers, "Because this is where the light is!"

Whatever the challenge, whether it is lost keys or a life-threatening circumstance, a common response is simply to ignore the facts of the matter and cast about for the simplest and easiest solution. Sometimes solutions are simple, easy, and right under our noses—in the light. But often we are denying the truth, refusing to acknowledge the circumstances as they are. This is the kind of denial which involves making a conscious choice, and it can easily become habit-forming. Repeatedly choosing to look for solutions in places where answers are absent becomes a pattern—a habitual response to the realities of life.

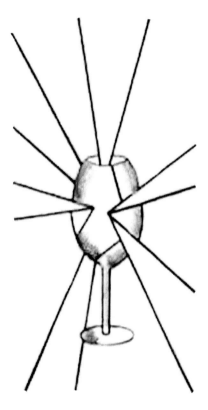

The real solution to the problem of lost keys—as well as problems encountered in our personal lives, our communities, and in our world—does pertain to the light. The mistake of the man in the story was to believe that the street light was the only light available. "Why not," we ask the man groping for lost keys, "bring the light to the problem?" Got a light? You bet! Virtually every spiritual tradition talks, prays and sings of bringing light into darkness. However, when facing a difficult circumstance, we, like the man in the story, tend to act as though the light is somewhere else—

out by the street, maybe—or perhaps in another relationship, another town, another job, another generation—anywhere else but with us. We are here to learn to bring light into our lives. After Jesus said, "I am the light of the world," he went on to say, "Whoever follows me will never walk in darkness but have the light of life." When we follow the light-filled way of life which he taught and lived, we begin to bring light into darkness, and we see the keys to life that were there all along.

There are times in our lives when we say, "All is lost." In our personal lives we lose keys, jobs, relationships, and loved ones. These are outer conditions and circumstances which can bring a darkness of such density that there seems to be no light–and apparently the end of the tunnel is not in sight. Unwilling and unable to see the light in these times, we tend to forget our part as carriers of the light. But if we remember to commit to bringing light into our lives, as so many have during the darkest of times, we realize that we lighten the burden of others as we enlighten our own lives. The light has a way of dispelling darkness around us, and more importantly, within us—revealing beliefs and thoughts that have been deeply engrained in our past and hidden from our conscious knowing. "That's just not me!" we will exclaim after repeating some uncharacteristic act or behavior, not understanding why we did such a crazy thing. If you have ever said that, or felt that way, don't feel alone. The apostle Paul, who spent a great deal of time telling others what they ought to be doing, also wrestled with

The eye is the lamp of the body. So, if your eye is healthy, your whole body will be full of light; but if your eye is unhealthy, your whole body will be full of darkness. If then the light in you is darkness, how great is the darkness!

- Jesus of Nazareth
Matthew 6:22-23 (NRSV)

Never are we nearer the Light than when the darkness is deepest.

- Swami Vivekananda

his own inner "shoulds." In his letter to the Romans, he wrote, "I do not understand what I do. For what I want to do I do not do, but what I hate I do. And if I do what I do not want to do, I agree that the law is good. As it is, it is no longer I myself who do it, but it is sin living in me. I know that nothing good lives in me, that is, in my sinful nature." Romans 7:14-20 (NIV)

Paul desires to bring the light into all of who he is and calls those parts of himself which he doesn't know, "sinful." Perhaps Paul is guilty, yet not to blame. When conditions become unbearable, humans are able to completely shut off—to completely deny—that these conditions exist. This goes beyond stories of losing keys. These are "keys" hidden in the collective consciousness formed of our human, cultural and family histories. This is the Shadow—skeletons in our psychic closet. We are guilty in acting out of our ignorance, guilty of denying that this is part of who we are—but to blame? I am not willing to blame Paul, others, or myself for that which is so deeply hidden that we have to ask, "Why do we do these things to ourselves and others?" Acts of terror demonstrate motives and causes so deeply hidden that we cry out in anguished confusion and anger, "Why do you do these things to yourself and others?" We know who is guilty, but where is the blame?

I understand that sin is just a word, a concept, but the importance of this concept goes beyond words to the very core of who we are. When we choose to label actions of our-

There are many sides of ourselves that we deny. We are frightened or repulsed by them and do not want to admit them into awareness. For ensuring our survival, we develop protective structures to defend against the power in those denied sides. We bury that power in the darkness, called the unconscious, and there we try to keep it safely out of sight. Our culture, too, tells us what is to be ignored, what is not to be done, and what is wrong. We dutifully store these forbidden areas in the darkness as well. A time comes in our development when we need to take back what we and our culture have put in the darkness because some of what we have buried there is essential for our next steps.

- Charles Bates

selves or others as "evil," "sinful," and "apart from God," we are expressing our immediate need for answers to the darkness of personal and collective Shadow. To say that nothing good lives in our sinful nature is to say that God is not there. Sin is our sense of separation from God. Sin does not mean that God is absent. I would say to Paul, to you, and to myself—as well as to those who continue to perpetrate the horrendous deeds so evident in our current news, that our journey as human beings is meant to deepen our understanding of who we are. We are here to accept and forgive ourselves and others. We are here to bring the light of understanding into that which we have called "sinful." We are here not to condemn, but to love. We are here not to deny but to accept ourselves. When I accept, forgive and love myself, I have allowed light to shine into the hidden dark places, the Shadow, of my soul. It is then that I deny the power of deep-seated beliefs and attitudes—rooted in past fears and nurtured in darkness—to control my life. This is not denying my true self. True denial means releasing my belief in the power of darkness and affirming the power of light to transform the darkness, the part of me which Paul called sin. When we transform that inner darkness, we are then able to transform our world. That part of our world which lies in darkness is more than ready for light. The conscious remembrance, awareness and acceptance of all that we are, and of all that we can become, is a choice to deepen and intensify our expression of light.

Whatever spiritual forces are, they have a dark side. While there may be only one God, God has many faces. Christ and Lucifer are twin rays ... Cain and Abel are two aspects of the same energy ... and I had very dark aspects that were not yet in my conscious awareness.

- W. Brugh Joy

To refuse the dark side of one's nature is to store up or accumulate the darkness ... Any repair of our fractured world must start with individuals who have the insight and courage to own their own shadow ... It is not the monsters of the world who make such chaos but the collective shadow to which every one of us has contributed.

- Robert Johnson

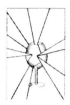

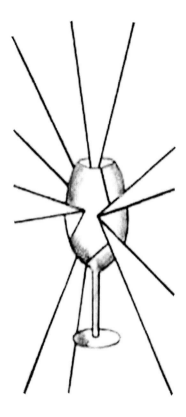

Break the Wineglass containing the belief...
"Out of sight, out of mind"
and fall towards
The Glassblower's Breath ...
"Nothing is lost in memory;
I Am the sum of my past"

Remembering: Inner Dialogue

How do I describe or define "the Shadow" in my own experience?

In attempts to work through particularly challenging or difficult situations, I may deny they ever happened, run from them, or obsess about them. Which of these options, if any, do I most commonly use?

Is there a more effective method of dealing with challenging and difficult situations than I currently use? How might my life change if I were to adopt this method?

Describe a personal healing experience which I consider related to the Shadow.

In what way did this experience involve "breaking a wineglass" (i.e., change my beliefs or perceptions)?

Remembering

Rule 3   Forgiveness

Completing the morning's lesson on forgiveness, the Sunday school teacher wanted to make certain that a major point had been made. "Now, children," he asked, "can anyone tell me what you must do before you can obtain forgiveness for sin?" There was a short silence and then, from the back of the room, a small boy spoke up, "Sin!"

You may have discovered during your childhood that certain apparently harmless activities such as chewing with your mouth open, or speaking before raising your hand, were often relegated to the category designated "sin." In another time or generation, playing cards on Sunday, or dancing, or wearing lipstick, would be considered taboo. Some were taught that it was a sin to go to church without their head covered. Others were told that it was a sin *not* to take their hat off in church. If the first requisite for obtaining forgiveness is that we sin, as the young boy in the story indicated, that would be easy enough to do. But none of these sins seems particularly unforgivable, and if they do mark the boundaries of acceptable behavior, they nevertheless are changeable with the passage of time and customs.

We talk a great deal about forgiving these sins. We ask, beg, plea, offer and "obtain" forgiveness for an entire spectrum of transgressions. But some of these deeds are considered so misguided as to be unforgivable. These

When a soul is encouraged to develop the mental faculties and to open the heart to a great feeling of love for humanity, it just naturally opens up the subconscious door that allows it to peer into the past. For before we are entirely free from the shortcomings and the ignorance of the race mind, we must awaken to the fact that these things exist and that we are connected with them, until through the Jesus Christ Mind we swing clear of them and establish ourselves in a consciousness of life and light and freedom and love ... Should we dwell upon such things, we should sink back into them. We must begin at once to rejoice in the light that is come to redeem our subconsciousness from the shadows of error and fear and superstition and mistakes.

\- Myrtle Fillmore

"unforgivable sins" are important to look at because they tell us a great deal about the limits and boundaries of our consciousness, as well as our behavior. These boundaries constitute the wineglass that calls to be broken if we are to fall toward the breath of the Glassblower.

We cannot grasp what forgiveness means unless we first understand what is meant by the word, "sin." I have frequently heard "sin" defined as "missing the mark"—a good definition that describes an action of being off-target, or making a mistake. A better definition, because it embraces a description of what is meant by being on "the mark," is this: "Sin is the sense of disconnection from God." This does not say that sin is *being* disconnected from God, but the *sense* of disconnection. When we act apart from our own or the greater good (God), we act as though we are disconnected, as though our actions have no relationship or consequences with others. But that is never the case; it is only a sense of disconnection, not the reality.

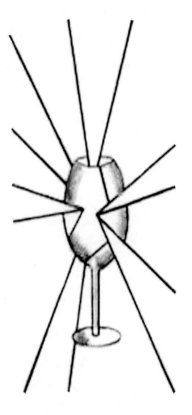

An even better and more complete definition of sin is: "a closed mind to the possibility of good." Think of that! A closed mind, a closed consciousness to the possibility of good, or to the possibility of God would come as close to unforgivable, and hopeless, as one can imagine. This is what Jesus meant when he spoke of sin during his ministry: "Truly, I tell you, people will be forgiven for their sins and whatever blasphemies they utter; but whoever blasphemes against the Holy Spirit can never have forgiveness, but is guilty of an eternal sin." Mark 3:28-29 (NRSV) The eternal sin Jesus refers to is not subject to changing whims and fashions of humanity; these are easily forgiven. The eternal, or unforgivable, sin is the failure to acknowledge or honor the connection with Holy Spirit, with God, with Life—with what we are referring to as "the Glassblower."

Let's consider this matter of connection and disconnection. What we think, or what we sense, may not be the whole truth of the matter. We may think that we are disconnected, when in fact, we are not. And the reverse may be true. One of the marked characteristics of religion over the centuries has been the tendency of the righteous "yes men" of God to blaspheme the very God they profess to serve. Thinking to be connected to God by saying "yes" to God, they are actually saying "yes" to disconnection. Jesus reserved his harshest criticism for the "hypocrites" and "vipers" among the Jewish religious leaders, who placed a higher value on the letter of the law rather than the spirit underlying the law. Destructive wars throughout human history have been fought with leaders of both sides proclaiming their special connection with God. The truth of all of us, however, is that we are each connected with God, regardless of whether we say "yes" or "no" to the connection. Picture this image in your mind's eye:

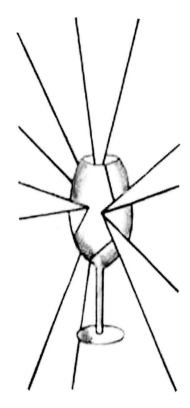

* There is a large, open field with hundreds of people in it.

- Each person holds a string, like a kite string, which extends high into the sky to a central place.
- There, high in the sky, picture God - however you choose to picture God. This is your opportunity! God may be a Woman, or a Child, or an Energy Field, or even a Glassblower!
- God is holding the ends of each string connected to the people far below. God is like a matrix at the center of converging lines.
- Notice that, from time to time, individual people are cutting the string that connects them with God. This act of cutting the string we call "sin."
- Each time a person cuts the string, God reaches down and ties a knot in the string.
- Notice that each time God ties a knot, the string is made shorter and the person is drawn closer to God.
- Forgiveness is the act of tying the knot in the string; tying the knot is healing the disconnection with God.

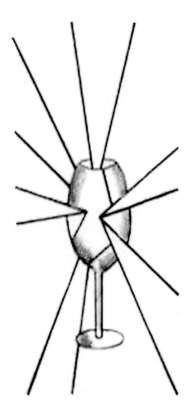

Who, then, is responsible for "tying the knot?" Who is responsible for the act of forgiveness, the healing act of reconnecting with our good? I once spotted a Marine Corps bumper sticker which said: "It's God's responsibility to forgive Osama Bin Laden ... it's our responsibility to arrange the meeting." With due respect to the Marine Corps, this statement demands some examination. It constitutes a wineglass which needs to be shattered! The truth is, it is our responsibility both to forgive *and* to arrange the meeting. God has given to humankind all that is needed to fully live life, represented by the image of the connecting string. When we choose not to forgive, we cut the string. There are some folks wildly running around the field with cut strings flying behind them—determined to be independent, to act alone. In the process they miss an opportunity for reconnection, forgiveness and healing.

In our connection with God, we are connected with our good, co-creators in this great creative process of life. To lose that connection, to no longer feel connected, is to feel alone, vulnerable and filled with self-doubt and fear. A midwestern farmer during the 1930's had fallen upon hard times. After a succession of failed harvests, he went to his banker in town and said, "I'm afraid, sir, I've got some bad news and some good news. Which do you want to hear first?" The banker replied, "You might as well tell me the bad news and get it over with." "Well," the farmer said, "I don't have enough money to pay my mortgage payment. I can't pay the loan on my machinery. I still haven't paid for the seeds and fertilizer from last spring, and the hailstorm just destroyed my entire crop of wheat." "My word," the banker exclaimed, "that *is* bad news! What's the good news?" "The good news," the farmer replied, "is that I intend to keep doing business with you!"

When we are enmeshed in the "bad news" of the circumstances of everyday living, it is good to remind ourselves of the good news: God

A minister parked his car in a tow-away zone and attached the following message to his windshield: "I have circled this block ten times. I have an appointment to keep. Forgive us our trespasses." He returned to his car and found this reply attached to his note... along with a parking ticket: "I've circled this block for ten years! If I don't give you a ticket, I lose my job. Lead us not into temptation."

on

intends to keep doing business with us. The
answer to the question, "Who *is* responsible for
the act of forgiveness?" becomes a bit clearer.
God's business—*and <u>our</u> business*—is forgiveness, the healing of severed connections.

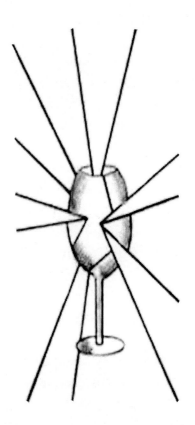

*Two monks on a pilgrimage came to a river
whose waters were running fast and deep.
Beside the river, looking anxiously at the
torrent, was a beautiful young woman. One
of the monks immediately lifted her onto his
back and carried her across. His companion
was scandalized. For several hours he berated
him. Had he forgotten he was a monk? How
dare he touch a woman, or worse, carry her
across the river? What would people say?
Hadn't he brought shame onto their holy
religion? On and on it went. The offending
monk patiently listened to the never-ending
sermon. Finally he broke in with, "Brother, I
dropped that woman at the river. Are you still
carrying her?"*

- adaptation of story from the Buddhist tradition

There is a great difference between forgiving
and forgetting. Truthfully, we do not forget
anything. All that we experience is retained, if
not consciously, then in the subconscious mind.
When we say, "Forget about it!" we are actually

saying, "Stuff it!" Stuff it away into some corner of consciousness where it sits, consciously dismissed as a low priority. The problem is that this "forgotten" incident, even though relegated to a dark corner of the room, still has an effect on the rest of the room—especially if it is smoldering or festering. Like a piece of old cheese, the smell can stink up the entire house. The monk carrying the young woman had not forgotten her, but the incident was past. He had released her. His companion, on the other hand, was allowing that incident to overwhelm his peace of mind, or his ability to experience the present moment. We have to wonder how many beautiful flowers, or delightful sights along the path are overlooked when we choose to hold on to the past instead of living in the present.

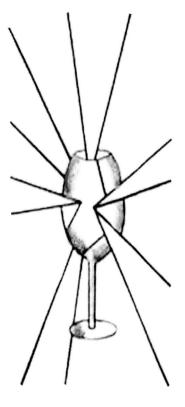

Rather than "forget it!" we would more accurately state our intention by saying "forgive it!" Forgiving is a conscious inner process which requires bringing light into the dark corners of the room. Forgiveness means being willing to remember, to see the past as it truly was, and to *choose* how to live with the past. This is a part of me, of who I am. How do I live my life now? The answer to that question is determined by the degree to which I am willing to release, let go—*forgive* –the hold that the past has over my experience of the present. What am I still carrying? Simply saying "forget it" does not lighten the load. Neither does simply saying, "I forgive you." Henry Ward Beecher once said, "I can forgive but I can not forget is just another way of saying, I cannot forgive." Forgiving others cannot take place until I have chosen to forgive myself. Jesus recognized the importance of this by placing it right in the middle of the prayer he modeled for his disciples: "… forgive our debts, as we forgive our debtors."

I must be for-giving up those debts and mistakes that I have accumulated over the years before I am able to forgive the debts and mistakes others have imposed upon me. The amazing part of this inner process of forgiveness is that when I clean my own house, it invariably decreases the need for forgiving others. The debts dissolve on every level—the inner consciousness as well as in the material outer world—"in heaven as it is on earth."

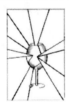

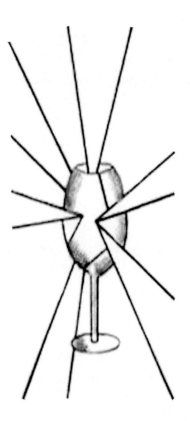

A man bursts into the old western saloon, frantically shouting, "Run for your lives! Big Jake's comin'!" Instant pandemonium! Everyone scatters, except for a newcomer sitting at the bar. An enormous man crashes through the door, tossing tables and chairs aside. He strides up to the bar and roars, "Gimme a drink!" The newcomer quickly hands over a bottle of whiskey. The huge man downs it in one gulp and then eats the bottle. Paralyzed with fear, the newcomer stammers, "Can I get you another?" "Nope, I gotta go,"

the giant grunts. "Didn't you hear? Big Jake's comin'!"

When Big Jake shows up in our lives, we have the same options as those available to the saloon patrons: *flight*, *fight* or *forgive*. With the exception of the new guy in town, who had no idea of the threat posed by Big Jake, everyone immediately opted for *flight*. Fight did not seem to be a sane option. In fact, when the newcomer met the huge man he assumed to be the infamous Jake, it was too late for *flight*, and *fight* did not appear to be a rational option. It is that third option—*forgive*—which is least used. The most effective of the three, it is also the most difficult because of all that old baggage—the doubts and fears accumulated and stuffed into the corners of our consciousness. In this instance, fear controls and limits options. In *every* instance, fear controls and limits. If not paralyzed by fear, we are at least restricted in our ability to be open to possibilities. It governs us to the extent that we see Big Jakes at every turn. This is not to say that *flight* or *fight* are never viable options, but to *forgive* requires putting aside the blinders and shackles imposed by fear, doubt, shame and all of those unnecessary patterns that we have accumulated from past experience.

Let's assume that I am that newcomer face to face with Big Jake. Neither *flight* nor *fight* seems to be a good idea. What does it mean to *forgive?* And how is it done? We have already hinted at the answer. Remember, Big Jake is really not who

Rule No. 1 is: Don't sweat the small stuff. Rule No. 2 is: It's all small stuff. And if you can't fight and you can't flee, flow.

- R. S. Eliot

A man goes to the doctor and says, "Doc, I can't get rid of this stink that always seems to follow me." The doctor asked what he did for a living. "I work for the circus," the man said. "I clean up after the elephants." The doctor exclaimed, "Why don't you find a new job?" The man responded, "What? And quit show business?"

I am forgiving. I am first for-giving up those beliefs and thoughts which hinder my ability to fully engage the present challenge. Whether "Big Jake" is a health challenge, a depleted bank account, or a pending divorce, the most effective and permanent course of action is to engage in an inner process of forgiveness.

When Jesus spoke of "agreeing with your Adversary," Matthew 5:25 (NIV) he was speaking of knowing and relating to the *inner* Adversary (in Hebrew, *Satan*). Consider that when Jesus encountered the Adversary during his experience in the wilderness at the very beginning of his ministry, he was alone. The temptations, distractions and diversions posed by the Adversary come from our own doubts and fears, from within us, not from some outer source. The power that you and I possess has little to do with changing or altering outer conditions—it has everything to do with changing and altering our perceptions of those conditions. This is the inner process of forgiveness.

When I forgive, when I engage in a true cleansing of my consciousness, I am more connected with the Source of my being, the Source of all. Paradoxically, this intensely personal, inner connection enables me see and feel more clearly my connection with the world and with others. When I am not forgiving I am imprisoned in a cell of my own making. I take the key of forgiveness and turn the key to open the door of my cell. I step through the door and look around

The "devil" is a state of consciousness adverse to the divine good. Other names for this state of consciousness are the Adversary, carnal mind, the accuser ... The devils that we encounter are fear, anger, jealousy, and other similar negative traits, and they are in ourselves. Christ gives us the power to cast out these devils, thereby cleansing our consciousness."

— Charles Fillmore

me. It is a different world. There are no bars or locks. I am a prisoner set free to be a part of a new world that was here all along.

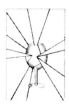

Beyond the physical act, breathing is intimately linked with a spiritual process. The very word, "spirit," is from the Latin *spiritus,* which means breath. Breath is vital to both our physical and spiritual life. Physically, we think of breathing through our lungs, even though we know that from our lungs, life-giving oxygen proceeds to fill all parts of the body. Think of breathing in a spiritual sense: breathing through the heart, breathing in the spiritual essence of life, which then fills soul and body. Have you ever thought of breath in that way? Take a moment right now—putting this reading aside—and consciously focus your attention on the breath. Breathe in the essence of life which fills your lungs and sustains your body; breathe out the used up breath that needs to be released. As you continue breathing, think of your breath as filling your heart—breathing through your heart. Now, choose to breathe in love; breathe deeply and hold...allowing love to fill your heart, your mind, and your soul. As you exhale, releasing the spent breath, consciously release that which you have spent, which no longer serves you, that which you are willing to give up. You are for-giving up all that is not loving. This conscious breathing is a primary spiritual process;

Since breath has such great importance, the greatest possible importance, it is clear that the way to bring order and harmony to our body, to bring order and harmony to our mind, to harmonize mind with body, and to harmonize body and mind with soul, is by breath. It is the development of breath, knowledge of breath, practice of breath which help us to get ourselves straightened out, to put ourselves in tune, to bring order into our being.

- Hazrat Inayat Khan

it becomes a prayer. Breathe in love, holding and allowing it to fill your being, and then breathe out—let go, forgive.

Forgiveness is a process that begins with breathing in love. It is a spiritual process; a very intimate and personal act. It is a personal connection with the Great Spirit of all life—with God, the "Glassblower." Rolf Jacobsen wrote of this connection: "I am the one you have loved for many years. I walk beside you all day and look intently at you and put my mouth against your heart though you're not aware of it." I become aware of the presence of this one who walks beside me, and feel the mouth against my heart, when I consciously breathe in love. Forgiveness begins right here—with me.

So often we think of forgiveness as forgiving *others*, forgetting the one who walks beside us, ignoring our own need for love and forgiveness. We tend to forget that forgiveness cannot come from a heart filled with hatred, fear and mistrust. Jesus understood this when he blessed those who are "pure of heart," and when he asked the angry men prepared to stone the adultress, "Who among you has not sinned?" He was saying, purify your heart, breathe in love, before presuming to judge another. It was from a loving heart that he was able to forgive the woman and her attackers. Breathing out forgiveness for others requires, first, breathing in love from Spirit. Breathing in love and breathing out forgiveness is not the prevailing climate in today's world, nor has it been in the 2,000 years since the time

"Forgive Your Enemies... If You Can't Get Back at Them Any Other Way."

- bumper sticker "wisdom"

of Jesus. But he staked his life, as have thousands of others, on the belief that this must take place if we are to be at peace. This requires a considerable shift in attitude, a change in perception. Most of us do not easily adapt to change because we are fearful of letting go of familiar ideas and beliefs. "Love is letting go of fear," proclaimed the best-seller published by Gerald Jampolsky several years ago. Exactly! Breathing in love leaves no room for fear, hatred, prejudice, or any of the other negative attitudes which we often choose in challenging circumstances.

If I turn my enemy into a friend, have I not slain him?

- Abraham Lincoln

"For years, I was neurotic, anxious and depressed," an acquaintance once confided. "Everyone kept telling me to change. I resented them. I agreed I wanted to change, but no matter how hard I tried, I just *couldn't*. What hurt most was my best friend also kept insisting that I change. So I felt powerless and trapped. But one day he said, 'Don't change. I love you just as you are.' This was music to my ears. I relaxed, came alive, and suddenly—I *changed!*" When my friend changed, his world changed. He was then able to love himself and forgive, rather than resent, others. The change which took place in his life required letting go of his fears, doubts and anxieties while breathing in love. He was not a particularly religious person, but he experienced a profoundly spiritual renewal.

Like the frog in the fairy tale which was transformed into a handsome prince when the princess accepted him as her partner in bed, so the inner enemy is transformed into a useful part of the personality once it has been consciously recognized and accepted as a legitimate and inevitable part of ourselves. For ...it is not the enemy who is evil but our unawareness of him which creates evil."

- John Sanford

If we are to change our world, we must first change ourselves—each one of us—*all* of us. I don't know about you, but there are plenty of times when I could breathe in more love. There are too many times when I choose to breathe toxic fear. Dwight Eisenhower once said, "Whatever America hopes to bring to pass in the world must first come to pass in the heart of America." We would do well to heed his words, as well as those of Jesus, or of the numerous spiritual teachers who over the centuries have urged us to look into our hearts, to breathe in love, and to breathe out forgiveness. Then—and only then—will we be at peace.

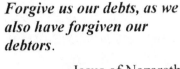

Forgive us our debts, as we also have forgiven our debtors.

- Jesus of Nazareth
Matthew 6:12 (NRSV)

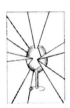

Break the Wineglass containing the belief...
"Only God forgives"
and fall towards
The Glassblower's Breath ...
"I am forgiven as I forgive
myself and others."

Forgiveness: Inner Dialogue

Who are my enemies? Is forgiving my enemies the same as giving up?

How is forgiving different than forgetting? When have I experienced that difference?

What was a specific personal experience in which I truly forgave someone or some condition? What belief or perception did I change or surrender before I was able to forgive.

Emilie Cady states, "There is no evil." If that is true, if God is good, and there is only God, why is there a need for forgiveness?

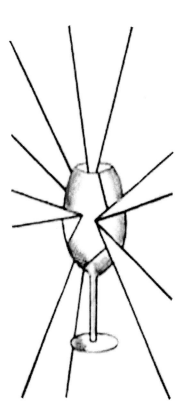

Forgiveness

Rule 4   Wisdom

Revelation will never come through the intellect of man to the consciousness, but must ever come through the intuitional to the intellect as a manifestation of Spirit to man.
- Emilie Cady

Several years ago, my wife and I took a trip through British Columbia—a trip which has been the source of dozens of stories. Most of these stories are true, and they are all improving with each telling. One of the most significant moments on our journey would have to be the time the river ran backward. This is certainly one of Carolynn's favorites, judging from the pleasure she derives from recounting the circumstances. I, on the other hand, do not find the story quite as humorous. That may be because most of the laughter is at my expense. I will have to admit, though, the time the river ran backward *does* seem to bring attention to some significant life lessons. So at the risk of losing a bit more dignity, the story bears repeating.

It is only with the heart that one can see rightly; what is essential is invisible to the eye.

- Antoine de Saint-Exupery

We found ourselves in a beautiful river valley outside Jasper National Park, just west of Mt. Robson, the highest peak in the Canadian Rockies. It was a gorgeous, warm day in July with flowers in abundance, and wild raspberries lining the banks of the mighty Thompson River—or what I *thought* was the Thompson River.

As we gazed at the picturesque scene, drinking in its serene beauty, I noticed that the current appeared to be moving in the wrong direction! The thought processes weren't moving too rapidly that day, so it took me a while to come up with a reasonable explanation for this phenomena. It must be, I thought, the brisk wind whipping up surface ripples. In retrospect, I would have been well off if I had kept this fascinating information to myself. However, I said, "Look, Carolynn. It looks as if the current is going north, but it's actually going south." Carolynn gave me her patented blank stare that accompanies any reference to directions. This gave me the opportunity to assume the smug, superior tone of voice that I usually acquire at such opportune moments. "You see," I pontificated, "this is the Thompson River, which flows south, and the brisk wind is whipping up surface ripples going north, so it appears the river is flowing north but it's actually going south." There was a long, long pause. Carolynn said, "No, the river is flowing exactly the way it appears to be flowing. There is no wind blowing, and if you will look at that small stream entering the river just beyond that clump of raspberries over there, you will see that when the current enters the river it is flowing that way. I don't know if it's north or not, but I *do* know that is the way the river is flowing."

I was shocked. Carolynn was coming dangerously close to entering my domain. I, after all, am a male. It is my task to know where we

Choose your rut well. You'll be in it for the next 20 miles.

- back country "wisdom"

are, how we got there, and how we're going to get out. This was becoming something of a point of honor, so I said, "I suppose I will have to get a map in order to explain this to you." And I did. There was a long silence as I intently studied the map, discovering that what I had assumed was the Thompson River was, indeed, the *Fraser* River. And the Fraser River flows north! My mind was racing. How to recoup this obvious loss of face? Carolynn was watching me carefully, barely hiding a small smirk at the corners of her mouth. There was long, long, LONG pause. And I said, "Well, it was an *understandable* mistake!"

Carolynn howled. She wasn't gracious at all. And ever since that time, the phrase, "Well, it was an understandable mistake," has become a familiar one that always makes me grin. It shows how easily we slip into the habit of making facts fit our beliefs. I believed we were seeing the Thompson River because the map said it was, and if the map said it flowed south, then it must be flowing south, in spite of all the evidence.

We are constantly reminded of how much of what we see is determined by what we believe. We leap to judgments based on our belief systems. It becomes less funny and more sobering when we recognize that our perceptions are shaped less by what we see than what we believe—not "seeing is believing," but "believing is seeing." What we believe, then,

Rationalism cannot conduct us to the essence of things. We therefore need intellectual vision.

       - Lasson

is critical in the determination of how we see ourselves and our world.

We all believe; we all have faith. The pertinent questions are: *What* do I believe in? *Where* do I place my faith? I may choose to place my belief and faith in outer trappings— other people, or groups of people, or political movements, or religions, or even *maps!* But I may choose to place my belief and faith in the inner essence of life. It is our faith in this inner realm which makes us whole and allows us to see clearly. Paul said that this faith is the "evidence of things not seen." Jonathan Swift put it another way when he wrote, "Vision is the art of seeing the invisible."

When all else seems to fail or is taken away from us, we rely upon this faith to take us through the dark, confused, or difficult places in our life. Faith brings us the energy, trust and inspiration to face and awaken to what is true in those places instead of running from them. We can be inspired by great books, by great teachers, by great deeds, but in the end, faith is found primarily in what is already within us. We use faith and belief to see what is true, to strengthen our capacity to open to the profound, innate wisdom each of us possesses. To believe this is to see.

There is ample evidence of the limitations of intelligence. More accurately, these limitations are not caused by intelligence but are the result

The muddle was so deep that for a time I was inclined to ridicule. Yet I couldn't get away from the evidence of a great power back of the flood of contradictory statements ... I noticed that all the teachers and writers talked a great deal about the omnipresent, omniscient God, who is Spirit and accessible to everyone. I said to myself, "In this Babel I will go to head-quarters. If I am Spirit and the God they talk so much about is Spirit, we can somehow communicate, or the whole thing is a fraud!"

- Charles Fillmore

The real voyage of discovery consists not in seeking new landscapes, but in having new eyes.

- Marcel Proust

of confusing knowledge and wisdom. Knowledge involves intellect, and wisdom involves an intuitive knowing that sees and knows beyond the visible and tangible. Both knowledge and wisdom require faith. Faith of the knowledgeable rests on the premise that "seeing is believing." But the faith of the wise ones requires belief in that which is invisible——"believing is seeing." This is the faith Goethe alluded to when he wrote, "Whatever you do or dream you can do, begin it." To follow your dream requires faith in a different guidance system other than the one with which we navigate in the outer world. We normally use our knowledge to negotiate passage through the physical challenges encountered each waking moment. But when we dream, or envision change, we move into another realm—that of the intuitive, or spiritual. In this inner world, reliance is not on knowledge, but on wisdom. Albert Einstein understood the distinction between knowledge and wisdom when he declared imagination to be more important than knowledge. He did not say that knowledge is unimportant, but he understood the primary role of the intuitive realm of ideas, the stuff of wisdom.

Every man takes the limits of his own field of vision for the limits of the world.

- Arthur Schopenhauer

Intellect is reading books, listening to lectures; wisdom is reading the book that is *you*—and each day brings a new edition! The role of the intellect is to bring and process information. It is the role of wisdom to discern the useful from the useless. Jesus, in speaking of the inner realm as the kingdom of heaven, said that it was "like a net," which, after being cast into the sea, is drawn back to shore and is then sorted—throwing away the useless. Wisdom is that discerning eye which allows us to perceive and know which of all the countless bits of knowledge and ideas drawn to the shores of consciousness are useful, and which to discard. Wisdom and judgment work hand in hand to process the knowledge brought by intellect. In the Sufi tradition, enlightened understanding has been referred to as the "wisdom of idiots." "Idiot" in this sense does not refer to ignorance, but to one who is different, or eccentric; perhaps one who would not hesitate to "break the wineglasses" of conventional wisdom. There is a Sufi saying that describes the relationship between intellectual understanding and intuitive wisdom: "The donkey that brings you to the door is not the means by which you enter the house."

It's in every one of us to be wise. Find your heart, open up both your eyes. We can all know everything without ever knowing why. It's in every one of us, by and by.

These words from a popular song are a reminder that in seeking guidance, we are best served by beginning the search with a reading of our own inner book. The shared wisdom of others may be helpful, but ultimately, determining what is mine to do requires personal discernment that can only be provided by my own innate wisdom. It's in every one of us. Follow-

O seekers, remember, all distances are traversed by those who yearn to be near the source of their being.

- Kabir

ing the guidance and discernment of our own inner wisdom is to place *be*ing <u>before</u> *do*ing, reversing the most common human response. Ordinarily, our doing proceeds out of our intellectual understanding and response. To act wisely requires going first to the inner place of being, and <u>then</u> acting—being proactive rather than reactive.

Work of the eyes is done, now go and do heart work.

- Rainier Marie Rilke

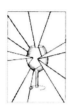

"You gotta have heart—
miles and miles of heart…!"
- Joe Hardy in Broadway musical, *Damn Yankees*

If, as the mythical outfielder sings, miles and miles of heart is all that is needed to succeed in life, why aren't we overwhelmed by success stories? Why do our lives often appear to be filled with setbacks and failures? What does it actually *mean*—to have heart—miles and miles of it? We experience heart throbs, heart aches and heart burn. We speak from the bottom of our heart, heart to heart, and if we want to get to the heart of the matter, we must open our hearts. Clearly, the numerous and varied meanings attached to the heart indicate a powerful attraction and fascination. The very word stirs a responsive chord within us, its meaning sensed rather than defined.

Hebrew scriptures tell us that God came to Solomon in a dream and asked what he most desired. The King James translation into English states that Solomon replied by requesting an "understanding heart." According to a scholarly twentieth century committee of translators, he requested an "understanding *mind.*" Come to find out, the King James version is closer to the original Hebrew meaning of the word "leb," which means heart. This word carried all of the meanings which we now attach to "heart"—and more. The ancient Hebrews believed that the heart was not only the seat of feelings, but also of mental faculties. True wisdom, then, required a marriage of feelings and intellect—an understanding heart. Reason, or intellect, is not enough. Understanding, without heart, is not enough. The French philosopher, Pascal, wrote, "The heart has its reasons which reason does not understand." We begin to understand a few more miles of heart when we link our understanding mind to the emotional heart.

It is the spirit in a man, the breath of the Almighty, that gives him Understanding.

- Job 32:8 (NIV)

The understanding heart is another term for consciousness, our *total* consciousness. It is important that we realize, when speaking of "mind," that we are dealing with all within our consciousness and not merely intellect. Charles Fillmore wrote, "At the center of the mind of every man is the light, the white light of Spirit." This brings us to the heart of the matter! At the center, the core, the heart of *each person* is the white light of Spirit. Many centuries ago this

I sought for God for thirty years ... I thought it was I who desired Him, but no, it was He who desired me .

- Abu Yazid (804-874 CE)

very same realization was expressed by St. John of the Cross: "There in the lucky dark, none to observe me, darkness far and wide; no sign for me to mark, no other light, no guide except for my heart—the fire, the fire inside!" Joe Hardy would have recognized the miles and miles of heart in that statement.

It is this light, this fire, which inspires and guides. It is this inner fire which moves us to take action. This fire within the heart is inextinguishable and inexhaustible. In ancient days guidance and direction were handed down from on high, inscribed on stone tablets. Just as the prophets foretold, however, there was to be a change. In the future, said the Lord, "I will put my law within them, and I will write it upon their hearts." This prophecy of Jeremiah was fulfilled when Jesus of Nazareth brought a message of change requiring a change in inner attitudes. This message emphasized turning to God within, in the secret closet of the heart.

There is nothing we can do which more effectively assures our success than turning to the heart, the inner wellspring of light, life and love. The understanding heart is an inexhaustible source of guidance, strength and peace. But circumstances and events in our world give ample evidence that we do not always follow the direction of our hearts. As challenges arise we tend to frantically go about the business of "fixing" them with practical, rational solutions. Differences between supposed enemies, as well

Thou hast made us for thyself, O God, and our hearts are restless until they rest in Thee.

- St. Augustine

I am not I...
I am this one walking beside me whom I do not see.
Whom at times I manage to visit, and at other times I forget. The one who remains silent when I talk, The one who forgives, sweet, when I hate, The one who takes a walk when I am indoors, The one who will remain standing when I die.

- Juan Ramon Jimenez

as designated friends, draw us into prolonged disputes. We tend to argue, shake fists, and sometimes even drop bombs, all the while justifying and rationalizing our positions. Conflict and war, personal or global, is not a product of the understanding heart. Meister Eckhart observed: "…in God, action and being are one. People ought to think less about what they should do, and more about what they are… though we are God's sons and daughters, we do not realize it yet." Being who I truly am requires being in my heart—with the I Am of me. This consciousness of the understanding heart opens the way to a fuller awareness of the unlimited possibilities of who I am and can be. The understanding heart is that place of wholeness within each of us where there is light. It is that place of fire which stirs us to strive for a more complete and loving expression of the inner Christ. When we live in the light of our hearts, we live in the light of God, and the world glows.

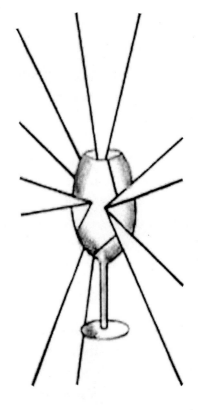

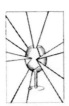

Break the Wineglass containing the belief...
"Seeing is believing"
and fall towards
The Glassblower's Breath ...
"Believing is seeing."

Wisdom: Inner Dialogue

When I needed guidance in the past, what did I do? Did I receive the guidance needed?

What does the affirmation "believing is seeing" mean to me?

What is the difference between wisdom and discernment?

In times of confusion and stress, what particular method or course of action do I usually choose in order to obtain answers to my questions?

Wisdom

Rule 5 Love

Ah, not to be cut off,
*   not through the slightest partition*
*   shut out from the law of the stars.*
The inner—what is it?
*   if not intensified sky,*
*   hurled through with birds and deep*
*   with the winds of homecoming.*

- Rainer Maria Rilke

One would think, after centuries of practice, that we would have perfected the art of loving. But it is apparent that is not the case. Stories of love become soap operas of love gone astray. "Falling" in love becomes the prelude to "fairy tale" romance. "Falling in love is falling in love with make-believe…," or so the song goes. "Fairy tales will come true, it could happen to you if you're young at heart…," another says. The love in fairy tales is filled with "ifs." True love will happen if you kiss a frog, or if the slipper fits, or if you slay a dragon. These love stories are filled with conditions, and when the conditions are not met, there is pain, sadness and often, tragedy. There is little difference between the love stories of ancient legends and fairy tales and those of current soap operas and movie screens. They are filled with tales of conditional love and, consequently, accounts of deception and betrayal. Comedians would go hungry if they could not exploit the stories of love gone awry in marriage. "Take my wife... please," Henny Youngman told his

There is no difficulty that enough
*   love will not conquer;*
No disease that enough
*   love will not heal;*
No door that enough
*   love will not open;*
No gulf that enough
*   love will not bridge;*
No wall that enough
*   love will not throw down;*
No sin that enough
*   love will not redeem.*
It makes no difference how
*   deeply seated may be the*
*   trouble,*
How hopeless the outlook,
How muddled the tangle,
How great the mistake;
A sufficient realization of
*   love will dissolve it all;*
If only you will love enough,
You will be the happiest
And most powerful being
*   in the world.*
- Emmet Fox

audiences, and he struck a responsive chord. The lessons of conditional, careless love seem to be lost on us. Clearly, the wineglass that contains our popular misperceptions of love needs to be broken.

Jesus made the distinction between careless and caring love. He spoke to his disciples of love when he said, "Love one another as I have loved you..." and he added later, "I do not give to you as the world gives." John 13:34 & 14:27 (NRSV) The popular conceptions of love seen in our soap operas are very different than the love Jesus described. He helped us consider misperceptions of love held in mind. In a sense, he proposed a toast of the new wine: "Here! Drink of this new wine, the wine of love." The love which Jesus proposed to his disciples required a shift in perception. Rather than "falling" into a state of conditional love, he urged us to "return" to a permanent and lasting love. He proposed a return which Rilke describes as the "homecoming." The world's perception of love has been shaped by experiencing disconnection and separation from the intense meaning and spiritual connection found at the heart of love. "Ah, not to be cut off," Rilke writes. We allow ourselves to be cut off and separated from others when we fail to connect with our own inner meaning—the *I Am* of who I am—not falling into love, but rather, *being* in love. The true stories of love well up from the heart. These love stories are essentially expressed

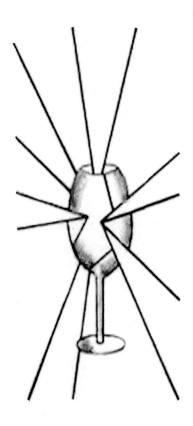

and experienced as poetry, as music, as friend-ship, as beauty, as life. It is this awareness of the all-encompassing nature of love that moved an early Christian writer to state simply, "God is love."

There is no fear in love, but perfect love casts out fear; for fear has to do with punishment, and whoever fears has not reached perfection in love.

- I John 4:18 (NRSV)

Love, like God, is both noun and verb. Like a magnet, love has an invisible and irresistible energy that not only attracts, but can also repel. Perhaps the most important aspect of this repellant power of love is in relationship to fear—"perfect love casts out fear." Perfect love is that love about which Jesus spoke, not the conditional love portrayed in soap operas. To fear an external condition or situation has the effect of giving it power. When we are afraid, we give our attention to the external, to the world, making it our priority. We forget to love, once again discon-necting from the source.

When Wisdom and Love are unified in the individual consciousness, man is a master of ideas and brings forth under the original creative law.

- Charles Fillmore

There was once an ambitious farmer who bought a new, highly recommended variety of corn seed. The results were so promising that his astonished neighbors asked him to sell them a portion of the new seed. But the farmer, afraid of losing his competitive edge, refused. The next year, the harvest was good, but not nearly as productive. The third year's harvest was even worse, and the farmer could not determine the cause of the diminished yield. It finally dawned on him, after a fourth year of diminishing crops, that his prize corn was being pollinated by the inferior grade of corn from his neighbors' fields.

The key word in this story of the farmer and his prize corn is *fear*. Ordinarily, we think of love in terms of personal relationships, but in this instance, we can see that the farmer's love was for profit, or his "competitive edge." His fear blinded him to following the course of truly loving. Such a course would have provided a different ending to the story, one that would have involved prosperity for his neighbors and himself. Emmet Fox once wrote, "Wisdom is the perfect blending of intelligence and love." The farmer had the intelligence to perceive the high quality of seed, but fear blocked his ability to share with others, to love others. What he loved most was profit, and, just as Goethe promised, this love shaped and formed his world.

"We are shaped and fashioned by what we love."

- Johann Wolfgang von Goethe

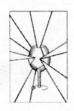

Where there is hatred, let me sow love. Where there is injury, pardon. Where there is doubt, faith.

- St. Francis of Assisi

My flight was right on schedule, and we were due to touch down at the Kansas City airport around midnight. The pilot informed us that the temperature was well below freezing and that winds were brisk. This was the last leg of the journey, the end of a long day. All that remained was to pick up the rental car and make the hour-long trip across the city to my hotel. I would be collapsing into the hotel bed by 1:00 a.m., getting several hours of sleep before making it to the 8:00 a.m. business meeting that morning.

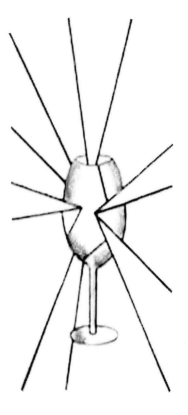

Everything was going according to plan as I lined up at the rental car agency desk. There were just a few of us—midnight in mid-January at the Kansas City airport is not a tourist's delight! The clerk had all my information on her computer screen. I handed her my credit card and driver's license. She hesitated, then said, "Sir, I cannot rent you an automobile. Your driver's license expired last week." Stunned, I went into instant denial. "No," I said, "that can't be. I *have* to have a car. It's the middle of the night, we're in the middle of a Midwestern deep freeze, and I've *got* to have a car." The woman very patiently explained, "You don't understand, sir. I *can't*

issue a car to you. It's illegal. I would be breaking the law."

Looking closely at my driver's license, the expiration date clearly showed that it had, indeed, expired on my birthdate—one week prior. Perhaps another tactic would work—passing the blame. "It must be the DMV's mistake. They always send a renewal notice. I didn't receive a notice." The woman was sympathetic. She said, "Sir, it may be that the California DMV is at fault in this situation. But at this moment in time, I cannot, I will not, rent you a car."

I stood there for a moment, beginning to consider possible alternatives, none of which seemed very promising, when a voice spoke up from behind me. "I'll take you." I turned to look at the man in line behind me. "I'll take you," he repeated. "Where are you going?" "I really couldn't ask you to do that," I said. "You don't have to. I'll take you. Where are you going?" "I'm going to Lee's Summit. It's an hour's drive, all the way across Kansas City. Where are *you* going?" "Oh, I'm headed to Leavenworth." "But," I protested, "that's only 20 minutes or so from here. It will take you over two hours out of your way." "That's OK. I don't have anything to do tomorrow morning, anyway. Do you want a ride, or not?"

I did. The woman behind the desk was relieved to be free of a frustrated, troublesome

We cannot be fully alive until we express the love we have. We don't have to receive it from others. In fact, we can't receive love from others! We have no room for it. All that we can do is to allow others' love for us to be a catalyst for the release of our own love.

- Richard & Mary-Alice Jafolla

customer, and she was so moved by the gentleman's generosity, that she upgraded his rental free of charge and sent us on our way. I introduced myself to my benefactor, Kyle. For several miles we engaged in standard, introductory small talk. My part of the conversation mostly consisted of profuse apologies for the inconvenience I was causing him. The long drive seemed even longer. At one point, we had to make a slight detour because of road conditions, and I apologized for the Missouri Department of Highways.

Finally, Kyle said, "Look! I have just returned from my third tour in Iraq. I was there when we first invaded Baghdad. There was a time when my unit was stationed in the middle of the desert, and we lost contact with two of the men under my command. I took my driver, and we went into the desert looking for them. There we were, in the middle of the Iraqi desert, not knowing where to turn. That gives a person some perspective. Taking a little extra time to help someone find their way in the middle of the night on the Kansas City freeways? Piece of cake!"

About that time, we arrived at my hotel. I knew that Kyle had another hour and a half to drive. I asked him, "How can I thank you? Is there something I can do?" He looked me in the eye and said, "Just pass it on."

No one single person, church, or organization has got a corner on love, because love is a circle and circles don't have corners.

- David J. Seibert

So that is what I am doing. Since that incident, several years have passed, and I've told this story dozens of time. What a lesson! Kyle, an officer in the U.S. Army, in the middle of war, teaching peace. *Pass it on.* What is it, exactly, that Kyle is passing on? What is it that we are all called to pass on? Martin Luther King once said, "Nonviolence is absolute commitment to the way of love. Love is not emotional bash; it is not empty sentimentalism. It is the active outpouring of one's whole being into the being of another." It is that "active outpouring" in which we are called to participate. If Kyle can do that in the middle of Iraq, then I can do that in the middle of Kansas City. In our homes, in our communities, in our world, we can each commit to *Pass it on!*

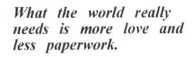

What the world really needs is more love and less paperwork.

- Pearl Bailey

Before Louis Armstrong became famous around the world, he spent a lot of time walking in his neighborhood on the South Side of Chicago. One afternoon he noticed a small crowd gathered around two street musicians. He stopped to listen and, to his delight, they were playing his improvised chorus of "Struttin' with Some Barbecue." At the finish of the number, Armstrong walked over and said, "Man, you're playing that way too slow!" "How would you know?" the musicians challenged. "Because I'm Louis Armstrong. That's *my* chorus you're playing!" The very next day the pair had a sign next to their tin cup. It read, "Pupils of Louis Armstrong."

Can you imagine how amazed Jesus would be at the incredible multitude and variety of improvised choruses on the basic themes of his life? Think of all the shopping mall displays, impressive places of worship, the very calendar system we utilize—all attempts to acknowledge the importance of his life. I can imagine Jesus saying, "Man, you're playing my song all wrong!" I reply, "How would you know?" Jesus answers, "I'm Jesus of Nazareth. That's my chorus you're playing!" So it is that we find cathedrals, churches and storefronts with their signs hanging out front saying, "Pupils of Jesus."

The challenge in playing the music of the master is that we become preoccupied and entangled in the notes and words *about* the music rather than just allowing the music to sing. That is how the love story becomes soap opera rather than a glorious and beautiful saga. The music Jesus sang is innate in everyone; he taught of a God as accessible to common folk as to the learned elite—perhaps *more* so because they have less to unlearn. The God which Jesus revealed to the world is available to all people in the secret place of the heart. Two thousand years later, some describe this place as being in the realm of the intuitive. But

Love is not a commodity to give, but a process through which you touch and express your own deeper nature. Love, then, is not the plaything of the emotions or senses, but the action of divine law.

- Eric Butterworth

these are just words and don't have a great deal to do with the music itself. This music of life is shaped by love, giving meaning and direction to human lives. This is the primary shift which Jesus helped usher into our world, the shift from seeing God apart *from* us, to God as a part *of* us. Because this is so, we are able to see ourselves as no longer separate from God, no longer separate from one another—we are linked together, interconnected—part of one great symphony.

Love, the inner music of the soul which draws us deeper, has a quality that causes wonder and expands our awareness. In a paradoxical way, the movement more deeply into the inner, personal place of the human heart causes an expansive awareness of the connection with all. This is exactly what Jesus attempted to convey when he spoke of being one with God, even though God was far greater than he—and his listeners scratched their heads and said, "Could you say that again? A little more *clearly* this time?" The writer of the Gospel of John wrote that Jesus said, "Oh, there's much more that I want to tell you, but you can't understand it now. But don't worry. The Spirit of truth will be within you, guiding and instructing you."

Here we are, 2000 years later, still trying to understand what he was telling us. It appears that we may well be at that point in the evolution of human consciousness when we

Someday, after we have mastered the winds, the waves, the tides, and gravity, we shall harness for God the energies of Love. Then for the second time in the history of the world, man will have discovered fire.

- Teilhard de Chardin

are ready to trust the Spirit of truth, to participate fully in the interplay between the personal, inner Spirit and the transpersonal, outer world. The disintegration of traditional political, economic and religious systems and the corresponding movement toward an internet-oriented global village vividly demonstrates this dynamic. Those who have a darker view of this new world tend to see human beings as impersonal units, cogs in a collective whole. The music Jesus sang had a far brighter and more enlightening theme. A song sung in some Christian traditions, "Lord of the Dance," conveys this vision. Jesus' worldview, or more accurately, cosmic-view, held that when individuals fully express love, the music of the heart, they become active and willing participants in the dance of life. The collective human body is transformed into an interactive and dynamic community.

You and I may stand on our respective street corners, playing our own versions of the tunes we love, and we may continue to think, "What a unique and special song this is!" But truthfully, each of us is spinning a version of the timeless music that flows from the soul's yearning to express the fullness and beauty of life. No matter how often, or how many different variations of the music of love we hear, its beauty and depth invariably move and inspire us. When we encounter a newborn child, a moment of shared compassion, a loving embrace, the music stirs us to laughter, tears, or, perhaps, thoughtful remembrance. And Jesus might say, "How beautifully you're playing my song!"

We unaccustomed to courage,
*   exiles from delight,*
Live coiled in shells of
*   loneliness,*
Until love leaves its high,
*   holy temple,*
And comes into our sight
*   To liberate us into life.*
Love arrives, and in its train
*   come ecstacies.*
Old memories of pleasure,
Ancient histories of fame.
Yet, if we are bold,
Love strikes away the chains
*   of fear from our souls.*
We are weaned from timidity,
In the flush of love's light
*   we dare be brave,*
And suddenly we see that love
*   costs all that we are*
And all that we hope to be;
Yet, it is only love which
*   sets us free.*

- Maya Angelou

Choose a job you love, and you
will never have to work a day
in your life.

- Confucius (551-479 BCE)

Break the Wineglass containing the belief . . .
*   "If I am good, I will be loved"*
*   and fall towards*
The Glassblower's Breath . . .
*   "I Am love and loved as I love others."*

Love: Inner Dialogue

What is this thing called "Love"?

What keeps *me* from loving?

What is the relationship between guidance and love?

What is the relationship between healing and love?

What is the relationship between prosperity and love?

When have I felt most loved? Was that also a time of feeling most loving?

When have I felt most *un*loved? How did I escape that state of mind?

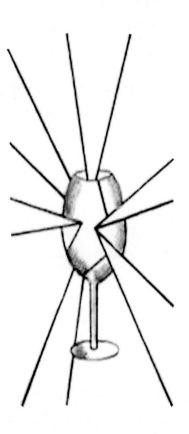

Rule 6   Waging Peace

There is a commonly held belief that human beings throughout history have experienced more times of war than of peace. I once heard a speaker carry this belief even further by stating that there has never been a time in history when war had not been waged somewhere on the planet. I suppose a case could be made for that belief, but there are several questions to be answered, especially if it is assumed that war is a natural condition of human existence. The statement, "It's always been like this in the past, so there's no avoiding war," easily translates to "Let's get ready for the war." Rather than, "Ain't gonna study war no more," the song becomes, "Gonna study war forevermore." According to this mindset, because humans are flawed, we will always be at war.

The problem with this assumption, which is understandable when we consider the impact of the accumulated pain and suffering of past wars, is that it limits our consideration of alternatives. I am reminded of the story of a husband and wife whose marriage consisted of one battle after another. There was constant bickering, nagging and arguing between the two. This state of war within the household went on for years. Finally, during one particularly bitter exchange, the wife had had enough. She stormed out of the room, got a suitcase, and began packing her clothes.

The God of Moses Speaks:
If in spite of these things you do not accept my correction but continue to be hostile toward me, I myself will be hostile toward you and will afflict you for your sins seven times over. And I will bring the sword upon you to avenge the breaking of the covenant. When you withdraw into your cities, I will send a plague among you, and you will be given into enemy hands.

– Leviticus 26:23-25 (NIV)

Proclaim this among the nations: Prepare for war! Rouse the warriors! Let all the fighting men draw near and attack. Beat your plowshares into swords and your pruning hooks into spears. Let the weakling say, "I am strong!" Come quickly, all you nations from every side, and assemble there. Bring down your warriors, O Lord!

– Joel 3:10 (NIV)

"What are you doing?" the husband demanded. "What does it look like I'm doing?" she fumed. "I can't stand this constant battling and abuse. I'm leaving home and good riddance." With that she stomped out of the house, slamming the door behind her. The husband stood for a moment in stunned bewilderment. Then he ran out the door yelling, "Hey! Wait for me. I'll pack my bags and go with you!"

How do we walk out on the near-constant state of war in which we find ourselves enmeshed? How can we wage peace rather than war? Is it possible? The answer is simply, "Yes." We wage peace by not allowing the past to define the future. We need to consider that there has never been a time when peace was not present. In the midst of the darkest wars, in the fiercest heat of battle, humans have expressed peace. There has never been *total* war, just as there has never been total peace. Before accepting that there has always been war, we must also accept that there has always been peace. In his best-selling book, *The Things They Carried,* Tim O'Brien writes of combat experience in Vietnam. A passage in his narrative eloquently captures the paradox of war and peace coexisting on the field of battle:

> "To generalize about war is like generalizing about peace... At its core, perhaps, war is just another name for death, and yet any soldier

will tell you, if he tells the truth, that proximity to death brings with it a corresponding proximity to life ... In the midst of evil you want to be a good man. You want decency. You want justice and courtesy and human concord ... There is a kind of largeness to it, a kind of godliness. Though it's odd, you're never more alive than when you're almost dead. You recognize what's valuable. Freshly, as if for the first time, you love what's best in yourself and in the world, all that might be lost."

As O'Brien states, "In the midst of evil," there is the desire for decency, for justice—and for peace. We wage peace when we acknowledge its presence in every circumstance, even those named evil. The wages of war are death; the wages of peace are love. When we wage peace we are loving what is best in ourselves and in the world.

Peace can be waged in an outer way. There are many organizations and groups that offer opportunities to express what is best in ourselves. There is an organization, for example, called Roots of Peace that has taken responsibility for clearing land mines from former war zones. This is no easy task. Recently, a land mine dated 1871 was dug up in France, so the destruction of past wars is still very much a part of our present. Roots of Peace is working to transform Croatian

"Put your sword back in its place," Jesus said to him, "for all who draw the sword will die by the sword."

– Matthew 26:52 (NIV)

Settle matters quickly with your adversary who is taking you to court. Do it while you are still with him on the way, or he may hand you over to the judge, and the judge may hand you over to the officer, and you may be thrown into prison. I tell you the truth, you will not get out until you have paid the last penny.

– Matthew 5:25 (NIV)

Peacemakers who sow in peace raise a harvest of righteousness.

James 3:18 (NIV)

minefields into fields of wine grapes and is beginning a campaign to turn Afghanistan's minefields into wheat fields. Such efforts are important to bringing about a more peaceful world, but there are other deep and certain ways to wage peace, ways that require personal, and therefore spiritual, commitment.

We don't often think of an inner practice as "doing" something. When faced with a difficult situation, people often say, "I don't know what to do. I guess there's nothing left to do but pray." Acting as if prayer is not really doing anything, and praying only as a last resort, we ignore our own resources and make a minefield on the very ground of our goodness. We can instead effectively wage peace as we establish peace within.

Jesus, Gandhi, Martin Luther King, and others have recognized the dynamic power that results from connecting with the source of peace. A few years ago, the Dalai Lama recommended a simple practice to increase love, compassion and peace in the world. The four steps, outlined in the margin, provide an effective method for waging peace.

Are we willing to commit to this inner, spiritual activity in order to create peace within and, therefore, "on earth"? Or are we, like the husband in the story, unable to conceive of a life in which there is no turmoil and con-fusion? It's worth a try, isn't it? As simple

1. Spend 5 minutes at the beginning of each day remembering that we all want the same things - to be happy and to be loved - and that we are all connected to one another.
2. Spend 5 minutes breathing in - cherishing yourself; and, breathing out - cherishing others. If you think about people you have difficulty cherishing, extend your cherishing to them anyway.
3. During the day extend that attitude to everyone you meet. Practice cherishing the "simplest" person, as well as the "important" people in your life; cherish the people you love and the people you dislike.
4. Continue this practice no matter what happens or what anyone does to you.

- Dalai Lama

as it is, there is no more effective action that we can take in waging peace than spending ten minutes with this meditation. Each of us can insure that the promise of peace is fulfilled within us, around us, and beyond us. And there will be peace on earth, as there is in heaven.

Living is a process that involves change. Being at peace with myself requires recognizing that change is necessary to life— change in outer conditions as well as in my inner, personal life. "I am at peace with the process" is a good, all-purpose affirmation for virtually all circumstances. Rudolph Steiner once wrote, "Man is not a being who stands still, he is a being in the process of becoming. The more he enables himself to become, the more he fulfills his true mission." As we recognize our part in the process of becoming all that we are destined to be, we come to an awareness of the beauty inherent in the changes of life.

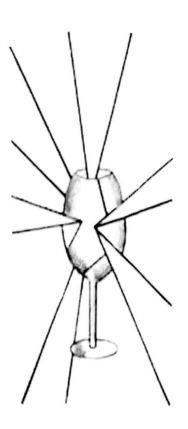

To meet changes with willingness rather than foreboding requires an attitude that sees life as a process in which we have an active part to play. It is true that encouraging and welcoming changes into our lives involves taking risks. So often, I feel stuck or "in a rut"

because I am waiting for things to happen *to* me or *for* me. Abraham Lincoln once said, "Things may come to those who wait…but only the things left over from those who hustle." Jesus emphasized the same message in his story of a man who, before embarking upon a journey, left his resources in the care of three servants. He entrusted one with five talents (a talent was roughly the equivalent of 15 years of a laborer's wage). To the second he entrusted two talents, and to the third, one talent. While the master was gone, the first two invested the talents he had given them. The third, who had received only one, dug a hole and buried it. When the master of the house returned, he praised the first two. When the third servant stepped forward with his one talent, he explained that he had been afraid to risk losing it. The master rebuked him in no uncertain terms. In this parable, Jesus emphasized that our gifts and talents are to be *used;* that to hoard our talents because of fear or uncertainty is to insure no rewards. Growth requires change; change invites risk—not a blind risk, but risk that comes from our inner-most being. These guided risks involve following the inner urging, which a teacher of mine once called "the divine itch." Getting out of the ruts in which we find ourselves requires a commitment to growth and change, a commitment that in turn brings excitement to life, a sense of peace and fulfillment. Mark Twain advised, "Take your mind out every now and then and dance on it. It is getting all

The source of my suffering and loneliness is deep in my heart. This is a disease no doctor can cure. Only Union with the Friend can cure it.

- Rabia (717-801 CE)

Don't be afraid to go out on a limb. That's where the fruit is.

- Anonymous

caked up." Paul of Tarsus phrased it a bit differently in his letter to the Romans: "Do not be conformed to this world, but be transformed by the renewing of your minds." Romans 12:2 (NRSV)

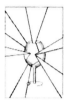

"For everything there is a season, and a time for every matter under heaven," the familiar passage from Hebrew scripture tells us; there is even "a time for war, and a time for peace." The ancient scripture speaks directly to the urgent questions of today: "How can God be present in the midst of confusion and pain?" "How can a loving God allow so much conflict and war-fare?" The Preacher of Ecclesiastes tells us that God is in every thing, in every situation, in every condition, in every human being. God is in that which we name "bad" as well as that which we name "good." When we point fingers, when we blame, when we judge others to be apart from God, we set ourselves apart— ignoring our own responsibility as part of the whole. In God's world, the Preacher says, there is both violence and peace, weeping and laugh-ter, destruction and construction. Ours is a marvelous world filled with dynamic polarities and paradoxes. The human responsibility is to be part of the whole—the *holy*—process. The holy scriptures of every culture are filled with

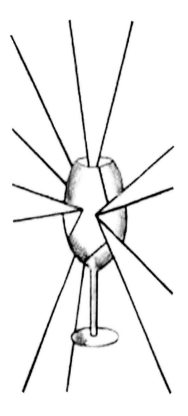

references to polarities like yin and yang, Shakti and Shiva. Jesus of Nazareth, who said, "Blessed are the peacemakers," also said, "I have not come to bring peace, but a sword." A time for every purpose....

I carry within me aspirations for peace as well as a propensity to violence. We humans carry this polarity individually and collectively. I do myself and others a grave disservice when I ignore these forces of creation and destruction. The inspiring and healing stories that come out of places and events—Jerusalem, the World Trade Center, Baghdad, Oklahoma City, Kabul—are invariably overshadowed by accounts of violence and destruction. But God is there, and God's good is expressing through every act of humanity as we express our individual perceptions of justice. The choice and purpose for each of us is to reconcile the powerful tendencies to create and destroy; it is in this reconciliation that we are healed and made whole, and become expressions of, as well as emissaries for, a true peace.

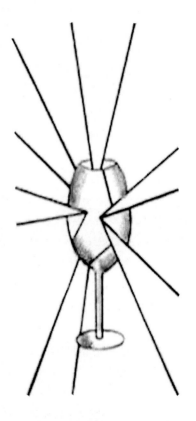

Peace I leave with you; my peace I give you.
I do not give to you as the world gives.
— Jesus of Nazareth
John 14:27 (NRSV)

When Jesus spoke these words, he contrasted a materialistic way of life based on rules of the outer, physical world, and a way of life based on inner, spiritual principle. *My* peace, he was saying, is peace that expresses into the world, not a peace imposed or established by others. Do not look to others for your peace, but find your peace within your own heart. I imagine he would have felt comfortable joining in a chorus of the familiar song: "Let there be peace on earth, and let it begin with me."

The challenge is this: How can I be at peace when all around me there is so much evidence of conflict and violence? According to the World Health Organization, forty million children under the age of fifteen are victims of family abuse or neglect serious enough to require medical attention. A recent study conducted under the auspices of the United Nations estimated that 45,000 to 50,000 women and children are smuggled into the United States each year, with violations of human rights ranging from slavery to criminal economic exploitation. Intimate violence, based on studies done by a national survey conducted by the Commonwealth Fund and a UNICEF study, is the single largest cause of injury to women in the United States, as well as worldwide.

But there are many who either deny the existence of this violence, or justify it on the grounds of tradition. For most of recorded history, parental violence against children, and men's violence against their wives, was either explicitly or implicitly condoned. Under English Common Law, which evolved during a time when monarchs maintained their

The most appalling cruelties are committed by apparently virtuous governments in expectation of a great good to come, never learning that the evil done now is the sure destroyer of the expected good.

- Katherine Anne Porter

rule through fear and force, even extreme parental violence against children was lawful, and husbands were legally permitted to beat their wives. Those who had the power to prevent or punish this violence through religion, law, or custom, openly or tacitly approved it. Some religious teachers still insist that punitive violence by parents against children and men against women is divinely ordained.

We ordinarily think of war and peace in terms of global conflict—great struggles to conquer and subdue others to submit to terms of peace. Peace through domination has been the way of the world for quite some time now. That way has been a resounding failure. General Douglas MacArthur stated, "I know war as few other men now living know it, and nothing to me is more revolting. I have long advocated its complete abolition, as its very destructiveness on both friend and foe has rendered it useless as a method of settling international disputes."

The means of settling global issues have a direct relationship to personal, intimate relationships. Throughout human history, the most violently warlike cultures have been those in which violence, or the threat of violence, is used to maintain domination of parent over child, and man over woman. We see this connection in the European Middle Ages, in Hitler's Germany, and in many religious fundamentalist cultures of today. It is a disturbingly familiar pattern. Yet, while there is much talk about economic

When I despair, I remember that all through history, the way of truth and love has always won. There have been murderers and tyrants, and for a time they can seem invincible. But in the end they always fall. Think of it, always.

- Mohandas K. Gandhi

and social factors behind warfare and terrorism, the link between intimate violence and international violence is still largely ignored. Often, we do not relate violence in personal relationships of home and school with terrorism and war, but if we are to build cultures of peace, we must look to the foundations of our most intimate relationships—the ways in which we relate to one another.

The all-too-familiar pattern in warfare, whether within the family or global structure, is to name the *enemy*, to demonize and shun the opponent, and to declare them *evil*. In doing this, we become more amenable to dominating and subjugating another. To read of this happening to people we have never met is one thing—to see it happening in our own homes is more devastating. And it *is* happening. The solution? A beginning point would be to ponder what Jesus meant by "my peace." Consider to whom Jesus was addressing his words—a select few? Or did he mean these words for everyone?

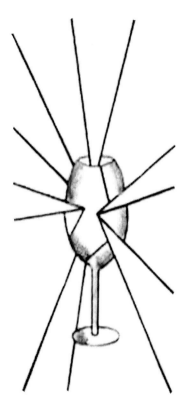

There is a story, related by Wayne Muller in his book, *How, Then, Shall We Live?* which tells of a tribe in Africa where the birth date of a child is counted—not from when they are born or conceived—but from the day that the child was a thought in its mother's mind. When a woman decides that she will have a child, she sits alone under a tree and listens until she can hear the song of the child that wants to come. After she's heard the song of this child, she comes back to the man who will be the child's father, and she teaches the song to him. The mother also teaches that child's song to the midwives and the old women of the village, so that when the child is born, the old women and the people around her sing the child's song to welcome it. As the child grows up, the other villagers are taught the child's song. If the child falls, or hurts its knee, someone picks it up and sings its song to it. W h e n the child does something wonderful, or goes through the rites of puberty—as a way of honoring this person, the people of the village sing his or her song. It goes this way through their lives—in marriage, the songs are sung together. And finally, when this child is lying in bed, ready to die, all the villagers know his or her song, and they sing, for the last time, that individual's song.

In that tribe, violence against one another—intimate violence—is unheard of. Each child, each person, is respected for who they are, a unique song of life. It works! A skeptic from our own highly technological and sophisticated society, wise to the ways of the world, may scoff at such a simple life. A question could be put to this skeptic: does your way—the way of the world—work? The challenge to us is to rekindle this simple spark of love in each of our hearts.

Peace begins, as the master teacher taught, within our own hearts. The song of peace is common to us all, even as it expresses beautifully in its own unique music. As we begin to

The nonviolent approach does not immediately change the heart of the oppressor. It first does something to the hearts and souls of those committed to it. It gives them new self-respect; it calls up resources of strength and courage that they did not know they had. Finally, it reaches the opponent and so stirs his conscience that reconciliation becomes a reality.

- Martin Luther King, Jr.

look for and listen to the song of others, in our families and in our communities, we begin to establish communities of peace. When we open our eyes, minds and hearts to these peaceful connections, we find that others are there waiting for us. In my own community, organizations carry names like SafeQuest, FISH, Giving Tree, Opportunity House, PeaceJam, Faith in Action, Child Haven, Habitat, Hospice...the list goes on and on. These are groups made up of people with understanding hearts. As we add our voices to the chorus, peace begins with us, expressing in a world that welcomes our song.

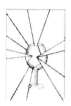

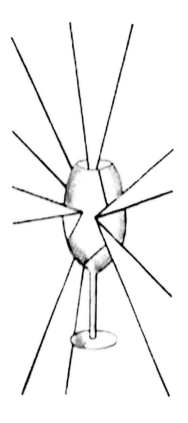

Break the Wineglass containing the belief...
"Others determine my experience of peace"
and fall towards
The Glassblower's Breath...
"I Am Peace...the Breath of Peace flows
in and through me"

Waging Peace: Inner Dialogue

In my experience, what has been the single most difficult obstacle to my feeling at peace? In other words, who or what is my Adversary?

What did Jesus mean when he said, "I do not bring peace, but a sword?"

When have I felt most at peace in the past? What can I do, or change, to bring more peace into my life now?

What am I willing to commit in order to promote peace in my life—in my home, as well as in my community?

Rule 7   Celebrating Unity—
the Oneness of Life

To see a world in a grain of sand
and heaven in a wild flower,
Hold infinity in the palm of your hand
and eternity in an hour.

- William Blake (1757-1827)

The town of my boyhood was virtually identical to dozens of other towns in California's Great Central Valley. Intensely hot summers helped provide both a ready source of conversation and the world's most bountiful agricultural production. Our house was right on the edge of town. Actually, the town was small enough so every home could make that claim, but in our case, it was literally true. The "city" limits would have been our back fence, if there had been a fence, and directly across the road was the "country," a world of vineyards and orchards.

Between the edge of our property and the road was yet another world—an irrigation canal. We called it the irrigation "ditch," or more often, simply "The Ditch." Everything of any importance happened in The Ditch. It was lined with blackberry vines that defied taming and invited exploration and development of secret tunnels and hideaways. Unwanted and discarded items of neighborhood households tended to find their way into The Ditch, where they were transformed into indispensable treasures with previously unimagined uses. It was

Last Sabbath I had a glorious time. Near the preacher's stand rose a great ledge of rock that overhung a small stream. It stretched for a half-mile or more. I went up to the top, gathered ferns and mosses, the most beautiful mosses. One's foot sunk down among them, green and silver and gray they were. O, to me the messages came then, from the Divine Spirit, more direct than through His human messengers! The good, simple-hearted country folk listened decorously to the man of God, while I, in a kind of charmed life, was part of all I saw, and a part of God. What have I said? But you understand me. You know there are times when we go out and seem to become a part of this great Spirit of the universe.

- Myrtle Fillmore

the place to be year-round, but the place and time most indelibly etched in memory is The Ditch in summer. Summer did not truly begin until that day each year when The Ditch would suddenly and magically be filled with clear, cold water. Later, I learned that officials of the Alta Irrigation District were actually the magicians who determined when and where to allocate melted Sierra snows into the veins of the Valley farmlands.

In our world, the coming of the water was an incredibly wonderful act of God. In the adult world, it was a source of worry. Concerned mothers painted dire pictures of bare feet cut on underwater debris, of drowning, of assorted snakes, critters and monsters—truth and fiction—to counter the irresistible lure of water. As summer wore on, the waters would recede, and at every level new wonders were revealed. Finally, the flow of water would stop altogether and only pools would be left. At that time, The Ditch would exude a distinctive odor, a smell which adults described as the stench of stagnant water. When I asked my father what "stagnant" meant, he replied that it was dead water. But I knew that was more adult fiction. You see, I was an authority on the world contained within The Ditch, and I saw plenty of life in the apparently dead water. I watched minute and squiggly little creatures called tadpoles grow legs and come hopping out of the "dead" water by the thousands! In the world of The Ditch, there was no such thing as death, only a con-

If thy heart were right, then every creature would be a mirror of life and a book of holy doctrine. There is no creature so small and abject, but it reflects the goodness of God.

- Thomas à Kempis
(1380-1471)

stantly evolving process of life. When the waters receded and finally disappeared, everyone and everything adapted. It might appear that nothing was happening, but that was far from the truth.

What a valuable lesson to learn! Isn't it ironic that years later, after accumulating the sophistication and knowledge of adulthood, I would return to a childhood world for the important lessons? We marvel at the ease with which children learn new languages or adapt to new circumstances. Because of their ability to focus on the present moment, they become totally absorbed and attentive to their immediate surroundings. "The moment one gives close attention to anything," Henry Miller wrote, "even a blade of grass, it becomes a mysterious, awesome, indescribably magnificent world in itself."

Since leaving my childhood world, I have moved through many other worlds. I have lived in cities—Dallas, Kansas City, San Antonio, San Francisco—and I have lived in towns with names like Santa Rosa, Vacaville, Wheatland. No matter what world I was in, large or small, the hopes, fears, dreams, and yearnings were exactly the same. I recall a conversation while living in San Francisco, widely considered to be one of the most beautiful and enlightened of cities. As I expressed my enthusiasm for San Francisco, a companion interrupted with the remark, "San Francisco is so

In nature, there is no such thing as a clash of colors. The more carefully you look, the deeper the subtleties of harmony. It is not so much that things flow into each other or around each other like perfect jigsaw pieces; rather it is that there is only One Thing out there. And, somehow, it is not really "out there." somehow, it is "in here" too. Inside. At the furthest wavelength of thought, the sea and the wind and the trees and sand are … me. It is a thought that blinks into the mind, like a giant laughing eye, and then is gone for a long, long time.

- Robert Hunter

provincial! You haven't really *lived* until you've lived in New York."

I smile at that memory as I consider the lesson from The Ditch. Like many of us, I have tended to place great importance on being at the "right" time in the "right" place, and I have wandered about in an unending quest for prosperity, or happiness, or enlightenment, overlooking the limitless presence of life around and within me, in this precise moment. The infinite possibilities and answers we seek are contained in the smallest incident and occurrence, in every event and circumstance. To see the world contained in a grain of sand, a wild flower, a pool of water, and within our own hearts is to see life in all its complexity and beauty.

When one tugs at a single thing in nature he finds it attached to the rest of the world.

- John Muir

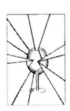

A human being is a part of the whole, called by us "Universe"—a part limited in time and space. He experiences himself, his thoughts and feelings, as something separated from the rest—a kind of optical delusion of his consciousness. This delusion is a kind of prison for us, restricting us to our personal desires and to affection for a few persons nearest to us. Our task must be to free ourselves from this prison by widening our circle of compassion to embrace all living creatures and to the whole of nature in its beauty.

- Albert Einstein

It was an ill-tempered and snarly group of about sixty tourists who spilled onto the docks at Juneau, Alaska, one early, bleak July morning several summers ago. Carolynn and I were among those who mumbled, stumbled and muttered all the way from the comfortable cruise ship to the cramped tour bus. We had been attracted to this particular tour by a brochure advertising a "Wilderness Experience." After the luxury and indulgence of the cruise ship, we were ready for an encounter with nature in its raw state. But this was just a bit too early in the morning, the bus was too confining, the ten-mile bus trip too far, and the boat destined to transport us to the wilderness of Gastineau Channel looked far too small and open for such an overcast day. It promised to be a crowded and chilly experience that would make a mockery of the anticipated encounter with wilderness. These thoughts were churning in my mind, and similar opinions and ideas were being bandied about by my fellow passengers. My wife was her usual, chirpy morning-self, but I was certain that fifty-nine other explorers on this boat were in for a disappointment. Not wanting to spoil her day, I brooded in silence as we cruised into the bay.

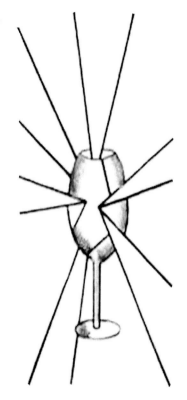

Then it began to happen! There were harbor seals, dozens of beautiful, graceful, shy creatures who kindly submitted to posing for the clicking cameras. Then came the porpoises, speedster show-offs of the sea, making passes at the boat in intricate maneuvers and formations. In their formal black and white attire, it was as if they knew their purpose was to delight us. And they did. The bald eagles, in treetop nests along the shoreline, struck regal poses, giving us their best profiles. I began to open.

In the middle of this command performance, the tour guide, rather nonchalant to this point, suddenly shouted, "Whale at 3 o'clock!" Sure enough, after working my way to the side of the boat, "Thar she blows!" This was a humpback whale, we were informed, distinguished by the arching of the back just before the deep dive preceding five to twenty minutes of intense foraging for food. But the best, most familiar, dramatic and beautiful part of the diving performance—always scoring a perfect 10—is the tail display. The tail, or fluke, is displayed by the humpback to announce its departure from the scene. The guide informed us that flukes serve to "fingerprint" whales. Even though the whales portrayed in countless paintings and photographs appear to be beautifully consistent, no two flukes are exactly alike.

Everything that is in the heavens, on the earth, and under the earth, is penetrated with connectedness, penetrated with relatedness ... God has arranged everything in the universe in consideration of everything else.

- Hildegard of Bingen
(1098-1179)

At the very moment this particular whale's fluke rose above the waters, silhouetted against a backdrop of forest and mountains, a sudden hush fell over the sixty of us glued to the rails of the boat. I wondered why tears were coming to my eyes until I glanced around and found that I was not alone in my awe. And for the first time on that morning tour, I remembered that I truly was *not* alone. Like almost everyone else, I had been so caught up in the incidental and trivial that I was missing the big picture. This "fluke" is not a matter of chance. Encounters with the wilderness are like that. They remind us of our connection. It is no fluke that people flock to those spots where they can glimpse life in its natural, unadorned beauty.

The stillness which we experienced together in the Gastineau Channel was an unforgettable and sacred moment. Each one of us who shared that moment may use different words to describe it, but we would agree it was a moment to be treasured, remembered and honored. The return bus ride to the ship was peaceful and serene. For the remainder of the cruise, a tangible and unspoken bond—a sacred trust—was established among those who had experienced the "magic fluke."

Often, in referring to treasures of the wilderness, we speak in terms of economic or political issues. Lines are drawn, and we are once again divided into grumbling, muttering groups who miss the larger, more important picture. Preserving the wilderness is not a small matter to be determined by political lobbies or economic interest groups. Name-calling diverts attention from the truth that we are part of an interconnected universe. I know so-called "redneck loggers" and "murdering hunters" who are as concerned and respectful of the wilderness as the most avid "earth cookie." We hold in common a sacred trust. The wilderness experience is a spiritual encounter stirring reverence and awe within the soul. The presence of the Creator is powerfully evident, powerfully felt, in nature. The part of us that seeks God, by whatever name, is drawn to nature for a direct experience. It is there that we discover the

When despair for the world grows in me and I wake in the night at the least sound in fear of what my life and my children's lives may be,
I go and lie down where the wood drake rests in his beauty on the water and the great heron feeds.
I come into the peace of wild things who do not tax their lives with fore- thought of grief.
I come into the presence of still water and I feel above me the day-blind stars waiting with their light.
For a time I rest in the grace of the world, and am free.

- Wendell Berry

connection we share with all of life, undiminished by time, distance and daily distractions. Nature's capacity to astonish, delight and enrich us is no fluke at all. It is our inheritance, our own deepest self, our link to the sacred mystery, beauty and perfection of Creation.

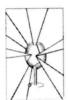

On my desk there is a small, ceramic tablet given to me by a good friend. It reads: "God is too big to fit inside one religion." Isn't that the truth? Religions, after all, reflect our perceptions of God, and these perceptions change. As our perceptions change, the face which has served to portray God in a real and meaningful way may no longer serve, so we cast about for another. This does not mean that past perceptions of God are inaccurate or "wrong," but that we are ready to see another face, another aspect. This became painfully evident when, as a young man, I found that I no longer believed in God. More accurately, I wasn't *certain* that I still believed in God. I came across a small book by J.B. Phillips titled, *Your God Is Too Small*, which helped me realize that it was time to look at God in a new way, to recognize that there are many—perhaps infinite—aspects of God.

The names we give God are attempts to verbally describe our perception of God. Jehovah, Father,

The most important commandment, said Jesus, is this: 'Hear, O Israel: the Lord our God, the Lord is one; you shall love the Lord your God with all your heart, and with all your soul, and with all your mind, and with all your strength'. The second is this, 'You shall love your neighbor as yourself.' There is no other commandment greater than these.

- Jesus answering questions of an argumentative scribe Mark 12:29-30 (NRSV)

Wakan Tanka, or Glassblower are attempts to name the unnameable. Perhaps the Hebrew insistence on refraining from speaking the name of God was wise, considering the limitations that one name, or one face, place on our under-standing. There are those who shy from the word "God" because, in their past experience, it denoted a judgmental and fearful entity who does not represent the goodness of life they wish to experience. If you are one of these, remember that whenever a shift in the percep-tion of God takes place, dissension and resis-tance has inevitably occurred. When Jesus of Nazareth introduced God as compassionate, intimate and accessible to each one of us, he provoked a reaction that cost him his life.

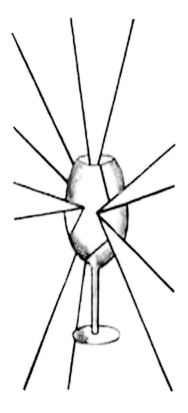

During his tenure of office, Abraham Lincoln was subjected to as much criticism and personal abuse as any of our nation's presidents. Not only political opponents, but members of his own party directed a constant barrage of slanderous insult and accusation at him. A member of his own cabinet even referred to him as "that baboon from Illinois." A reporter once asked the President how he could remain calm in the midst of such an onslaught. Lincoln answered him by relating the following story: "I once came upon a farmer who was plowing his field with the help of a worn out old horse," Abe said. "As we talked, I noticed a huge fly on the rump of the old horse. It was obviously irritating the horse, so I thought I'd help the hard-working creature. I leaned over to swat that fly. 'Don't you touch that fly, Abe,' the farmer commanded. 'That fly is the only thing keepin' this old hoss movin'.'" "Young fellow," Abe said to the reporter, "if it weren't for these folks swarming around me with their barbs and arrows, *I* might not keep moving!"

If it were not for the differing, and often disagreeable, viewpoints that pose challenges to long-held beliefs and opinions, we might become too self-satisfied, comfortable and more reluctant to keep moving, changing and growing. There is currently a significant shift taking place in human consciousness. This shift is not merely occurring in theological or religious views but in every area of human experience. It is part of the movement toward wholeness in medicine, in environmental science, in economics, in physics, and in politics. It is a movement away from separation, division and conflict and toward the holistic, cooperative community. In the spiritual realm, the shift may be seen as a movement toward honoring the feminine aspect of God. These shifts and changes often provoke discomfort and controversy. We typically do not enjoy having our wineglasses shattered.

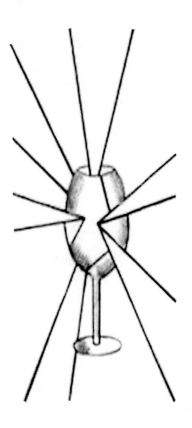

Whether we agree or disagree with another's perceptions of God is less important than what we do with our own beliefs. Often, differing opinions which annoy us serve the same function as the fly in Lincoln's story—they spur us into action, causing us to question, to clarify, and *sometimes* ... even to change our minds! This process expands our perceptions of life and increases our awareness. Perceptions of life, and of God, undergo constant change. In fact, the Bible could be called the most complete historical record of the evolution of human perceptions of God. Perceptions of God are changeable; although God has not changed, human perceptions *have!*

The Jehovah God of the ancient Hebrews was a war god. This God required the brutal annihilation of those who opposed Him. This perception of God was power-based, war-like, and dominated the era. "Eye for an eye" was the order of the day. This perception of God is being challenged today, causing discomfort and provoking argument. It is important to recognize that beliefs of others cannot be dismissed merely by labeling them "radical" or "reactionary"——"feminist" or "chauvinist." Jesus introduced a new model, a more compassionate, loving God. He clearly expressed the desire not to abandon old perceptions but to go beyond them ("I come not to abolish the law, but to fulfill it"). Jesus called us to expand our awareness, to see the feminine as well as the masculine face of God. For "those who have eyes to see, and ears to hear," as Jesus said, there is a growing appreciation of the differences between us, motivating us to integrate the masculine and feminine aspects of God in our individual lives and in our world. Our relationship with the Infinite God of Many Faces is

"...in the image of God were humans created; male and female God created them."

-Genesis 1:27 (NIV)

strengthened in this process, and we experience life more fully as we open to an appreciation of all of who we are.

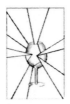

Yea, though I walk through the valley of the shadow of death, I will fear no evil: for thou art with me...
- from the 23rd Psalm, King James Version

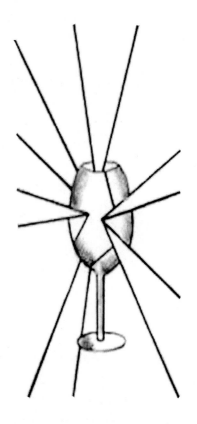

Several years ago, at the family gathering which traditionally took place at Thanksgiving, I realized there was something amiss. Ordinarily, family celebrations revolved around my mother. Although she would have denied it, she reveled in her role as matriarch. She would make certain, often against seemingly insurmountable odds, that everyone, including the turkey, was stuffed and properly dressed. She was, only half-jokingly, referred to as "the General." This came to mind as I observed the raucous, amiable gathering of generations at my sister's home. The General had retired; she was sitting in a corner of the room with a half-smile on her face, her eyes feasting on the familiar dynamics of kids and their parents growing up. In the several hours spent at the celebration, I didn't hear her speak more than a few sentences.   Only if you had known her before would you recognize what a change that signified! I was saddened that the mother I knew would no longer be with me. In a real sense, that mother had died. Somehow, just acknowledging that was a comfort. After that, I observed a new mother emerging, very much at peace with herself, more accepting of others. There was a sweetness about her not always evident in the past. She was having less trouble walking through the valley of the shadow of death than I. As she moved more deeply into the winter of her life, her clear intention was to live. The puzzling statement which Jesus made to his followers, "Let the dead bury the dead," became clear. She chose to live. We tend to make such a distinction between life and death, forgetting that death *is* part of the life process. There is death—and life—in the shadows of our consciousness.

The life experience which we label death calls us, *forces* us to consider how to walk through the "valley." Witnessing death calls us to remember and to move into the mysterious realm of spirit. Most of us have a belief, opinion, or faith regarding what happens after death, wanting to know exactly where, how and why we're going wherever we're going. I have my own beliefs and faith regarding ongoing life, bolstered and buttressed by scientific, psychological and theological evidence. But when all is said and done, there is no denying the sadness and pain that accompany the loss we feel at a loved one's death. At that time, speculations and beliefs are dead issues, and it is time to let

To men some things are good and some are bad. But to God, all things are good and beautiful and just.

- Heraclitus
(540-470 B.C.E.)

them die. The important question is, "How do I choose to live through the experience of death?"

When I am with someone who is preparing to die, they will often ask, "What am I supposed to do?" In the past I thought I was obligated to tell them what they should be doing. But now my answer to that question is, "Yours is not to *do,* but to *be.*" That may be an unsatisfactory answer to some, but it is my reminder to be at peace with the process—to remember that this is yet another experience of life. Hospice workers, and those who dedicate themselves to being with those involved in living through the process of dying, know the great value of just "being there." Being there, being present, opens the way to experiencing the peace that supports life. The lesson we are still learning is that life may express as physical healing of the body, or it may involve a transition into another form, which we describe as death.

Like many in our culture, I learned that death was something to be whispered about or mentioned in euphemistic ways such as "passing to the other side," or "making the transition." This is an attempt to avoid, ease, or forget the fear and pain. But I remember. We always do. I remember avoiding funerals, even that of my own father who died suddenly almost forty years ago. I resisted going to his casket, keeping my own children from being exposed to the "unpleasant" experience. I was a young man

Even though you intended to do harm to me, God meant it for good.

- Joseph forgives brothers who sold him into slavery. Genesis 50:20 (NRSV)

then and since that time have grown in my understanding and honoring of life. For years I experienced a sense of guilt and incompletion, wishing that I had helped to bury my father with the dignity and respect he deserved. Since that time, I have read enough books, attended enough seminars, and prayed enough prayers to know that the time has come to "let the dead bury the dead." I am no longer the person I was—that person is dead. It is important to remember the guilt and shame, and to move beyond shame and guilt into love and respect. This remembrance is a greater teacher than any book or seminar. If I commit to remembering through the layers of memories that lie in the shadow, I will come to the place of remembering who I truly am. The most important and profound teachers are those who allow others to be with them during their process of dying. The honesty and wisdom—the *sincerity*—which humans offer at this time is a true gift. When we remember to be with all of life, even that which we call death, we open ourselves to being the containers for healing and peace—and *that* is worth remembering!

> *To produce a man, there must be a combination of forces that at some stages of soul evolution may seem to work against one another; but when one understands that the great creative Mind brings forth under law, reconciliation and consistency are found where inharmony and contradiction seemed dominant.*
>
> - Charles Fillmore

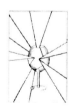

A friend of mine had worked for several years at the ticket counter of a major airline at the Los Angeles International Airport. There were frequent opportunities to experience the personal foibles of famous and near-famous people. Whatever the topic of conversation, she would revive these past encounters, invariably pointing out personal shortcomings and imperfections. She delighted in whittling screen heroes and heroines down to size. This seems to be the human tendency - to place leaders on pedestals and then knock them down. It is as though we lift them up so that we might get a better view of their flaws.

Marble is traditionally used in carving pedestals, as well as the human likenesses placed on them. The marble used for these purposes is selected from stones with the least number of flaws and imperfections. Interestingly, the word "sincere" comes from the Italian stonecutters who spoke of the perfect marble as being *sin cere*, "without flaw." A more accurate description would be "without *apparent* flaw" because the marble out of which the sculpture is carved is filled with fissures, gaps and impurities. As human beings, we all have these fissures—wounds and impurities—which are part of the human experience. It is easy enough to call attention to the imperfections of others, especially those who are most visible—politicians, movie celebrities, televangelists, lawyers. "This is the price of fame," some would say. But the price I pay for choosing to focus on the flaws in others is that I fail to see the flaws of my own being; I am not immersing

You have to be God and the devil, both of them. Being a good medicine man means being right in the midst of the turmoil, not shielding yourself from it. It means experiencing life in all its phases. It means not being afraid of cutting up and playing the fool now and then. That's sacred too.

-Lame Deer

No man is an island, entire of itself; every man is a piece of the Continent, a part of the main; if a clod be washed away by the sea, Europe is the less, as well as if a promontory were, as well as if a manor of thy friend's or of thine own were; any man's death diminishes me, because I am involved in Mankind; and therefore never send to know for whom the bell tolls; it tolls for thee.

- John Donne

myself in the sea of shared consciousness, and I do not know myself and cannot begin to heal myself or others. This is a high price to pay for my unnecessary judgments.

Choosing to focus on the possibility and reality of perfection rather than the appearance of flaws means to forgive myself and others, to love in spite of the flaws. This choice affirms the perfection of the spiritual essence within each one of us rather than focusing on the wounded imperfections common to our shared human experience. This is an important step towards healing, moving beyond vindictiveness and separation into forgiveness and love. When I do this personally–when we do this as a community and as a planet–we will heal our wounds and sincerely see the perfection in shadow and in light.

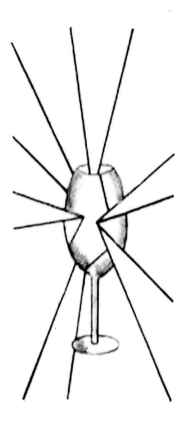

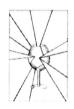

Break the Wineglass containing the belief...
"I am alone"
and fall towards
The Glassblower's Breath...
"I am a part of—I am connected with—
all life. I am never alone.
I Am!"

Celebrating Unity—the Oneness of Life:
Inner Dialogue

With which of the three characters - the father, the younger son, or the older son - in the parable of the Prodigal Son do I most closely identify? Luke 15:11-32 (NRSV)

Have there been various times during my life when I experienced being each of the three?

If there is only God—only good—is there a need to "change" or "fix" things? Why, or why not?

When have I experienced the deepest sense of oneness with all life? What do I need to do to experience this more often?

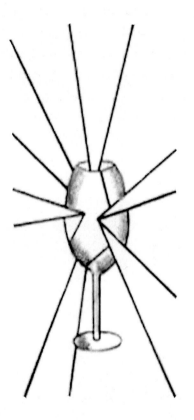

About the Author

Vic Jenkins received a Bachelor of Arts degree in music from San Francisco State University, a Master of Arts degree in history from Southern Methodist University, and graduated from Unity School of Christianity in Missouri as an ordained minister, serving for twenty years as a Unity minister in Vacaville, California. The diverse projects, classes, workshops and presentations in which he has been involved over the years reflect his eclectic interests and training. He has a happy knack for lessening the distance between peer counseling programs, baseball, Jungian dream work, gardening, and pit orchestras. Currently, he is living a full life with his wife, Carolynn, and two cats— deciding what he wants to be when he grows up.

Vic's website is:
http://vicjenkins.homestead.com/

To contact author or order more books see page 103

References & Suggestions for Further Reading

Willis Barnstone, ed., *The Other Bible* (San Francisco: Harper), 2005

Charles Bates, *Pigs Eat Wolves* (St. Paul, MN: Yes Publishing Co.), 1991

Wendell Berry, *Collected Poems, 1957-1982* (New York: North Point Press), 1984

Karen Blixen, *Babette's Feast and Other Anecdotes of Destiny* (New York: Vintage Books), 1953

Robert Bly, James Hillman & Michael Meade, eds., *The Rag and Bone Shop of the Heart* (New York: HarperCollins), 1992

Eric Butterworth, *Discover the Power within You* (New York: Harper & Row), 1968

Emilie Cady, *Lessons in Truth* (Unity Village, MO: Unity Books), 1903

Anthony de Mello, *The Song of the Bird* (Garden City, NY: Image Books), 1984

Riane Eisler, *The Chalice and the Blade* (New York: Harper & Row), 1987

Charles Fillmore, *Christian Healing* (Unity Village, MO: Unity Books), 1909

Charles Fillmore, *Jesus Christ Heals* (Unity Village, MO: Unity Books), 1939

Charles Fillmore, *The Revealing Word* (Unity Village, MO: Unity Books), 1959

Charles Fillmore, *Talks on Truth* (Unity Village, MO: Unity Books), 1926

Charles Fillmore, *The Twelve Powers of Man* (Unity Village, MO: Unity Books), 1930

Myrtle Fillmore, *Healing Letters* (Unity Village, MO: Unity Books), 1981

Myrtle Fillmore, *How to Let God Help You* (Unity Village, MO: Unity Books), 1956

Emmet Fox, *Around the Year with Emmet Fox* (New York: Harper), 1958

Emmet Fox, *Sermon on the Mount* (New York: Harper), 1934

James Gaither and Charles Fillmore, *The Essential Charles Fillmore* (Unity Village, MO: Unity Books), 1999

Matthew Fox, *The Coming of the Cosmic Christ* (New York: Harper & Row), 1987

References

Matthew Fox, ed., *Meditations with Meister Eckhart* (Santa Fé, NM: Bear & Co.), 1983

F.C. Happold, *Mysticism: A Study & An Anthology* (New York: Penguin), 1970

Robert Johnson, *Owning Your Own Shadow* (New York: HarperCollins), 1991

W. Brugh Joy, *Avalanche: Heretical Reflections on the Dark and the Light* (New York: Ballantine), 1990

Carl Jung, "The Concept of the Collective Unconscious," *The Portable Jung*, Joseph Campbell, ed. (New York: Viking Press), 1971

Hazrat Inayat Khan, *The Sufi Message: Health, Mental Purification & the Mind World* (Geneva: International Headquarters Sufi Movement), 1961

Stephen Levine, *Healing into Life and Death* (New York: Doubleday), 1987

Robert S. Miller, ed., *As Above, So Below* (Los Angeles: Jeremy P. Tarcher), 1992

Stephen Mitchell, ed., *The Enlightened Heart* (New York: HarperCollins), 1989

Wayne Muller, *How, Then, Shall We Live?* (New York: Bantam), 1996

Tim O'Brien, *The Things They Carried* (Boston: Houghton Mifflin), 1990

J.B. Phillips, *Your God Is Too Small* (New York: The Macmillan Co.), 1958

Sidney Piburn, ed., *The Dalai Lama: A Policy of Kindness* (Ithaca, NY: Snow Lion Publications), 1993

John Sanford, *Evil, the Shadow Side of Reality* (New York: Crossroad), 1981

John Sanford, *The Kingdom Within* (New York: Paulist Press), 1970

Idries Shah, *The Way of the Sufi* (New York: Dutton), 1970

Thomas Shepherd, *Friends in High Places* (New York: iUniverse, Inc.), 2006

John Shelby Spong, *Rescuing the Bible from Fundamentalism* (San Francisco: Harper), 1991

Connie Zweig & Jeremiah Abrams, eds., *Meeting the Shadow* (New York: Jeremy P. Tarcher), 1991

Book ordering information

Breaking the Wineglass... is available from the author at

http://vicjenkins.homestead.com/

or Amazon.com and Barnesandnoble.com

The publisher of Breaking the Wineglass,

is Ravenswood Court Publishing,

an imprint of James Stevenson Publisher

www.jspub.com/

CPSIA information can be obtained at www.ICGtesting.com
Printed in the USA
LVOW131123051011

249199LV00004B/77/P

9 781885 852496